Cambridge Elements

Elements in the Archaeology of Food
edited by
Katheryn C. Twiss
Stony Brook University, New York
Alexandra Livarda
Catalan Institute of Classical Archaeology

FOOD TABOOS IN ARCHAEOLOGY

Max Price
Durham University

Shaftesbury Road, Cambridge CB2 8EA, United Kingdom

One Liberty Plaza, 20th Floor, New York, NY 10006, USA

477 Williamstown Road, Port Melbourne, VIC 3207, Australia

314–321, 3rd Floor, Plot 3, Splendor Forum, Jasola District Centre,
New Delhi – 110025, India

Cambridge University Press is part of Cambridge University Press & Assessment, a department of the University of Cambridge.

We share the University's mission to contribute to society through the pursuit of education, learning and research at the highest international levels of excellence.

www.cambridge.org
Information on this title: www.cambridge.org/9781009663571

DOI: 10.1017/9781009663595

© Max Price 2026

This publication is in copyright. Subject to statutory exception and to the provisions of relevant collective licensing agreements, no reproduction of any part may take place without the written permission of Cambridge University Press & Assessment.

When citing this work, please include a reference to the DOI 10.1017/9781009663595

First published 2026

A catalogue record for this publication is available from the British Library

A Cataloging-in-Publication data record for this Element is available from the Library of Congress

ISBN 978-1-009-66357-1 Hardback
ISBN 978-1-009-66361-8 Paperback
ISSN 2754-2971 (online)
ISSN 2754-2963 (print)

Cambridge University Press & Assessment has no responsibility for the persistence or accuracy of URLs for external or third-party internet websites referred to in this publication and does not guarantee that any content on such websites is, or will remain, accurate or appropriate.

For EU product safety concerns, contact us at Calle de José Abascal, 56, 1°, 28003 Madrid, Spain, or email eugpsr@cambridge.org

Food Taboos in Archaeology

Elements in the Archaeology of Food

DOI: 10.1017/9781009663595
First published online: March 2026

Max Price
Durham University
Author for correspondence: Max Price, mdprice87@gmail.com

Abstract: Anthropologists have struggled with the concept of the food taboo for over a century; and archaeologists struggle with detecting them in the material signatures of the past. Yet by recognizing that ancient peoples must have followed taboos, some of which may have persisted for thousands of years, we gain insight into how cultural traditions shaped the ways in which people ate and interacted with their environments. This Element concerns food and the cultural structures that surround it. It provides an overview of the history and anthropological understandings of food taboos, and offers critical engagement with the current archaeological method and theory investigating these. Archaeological case studies, including the pig taboo in Judaism and ethnoarchaeological analysis of various mammalian taboos among the Nukak of Amazonia, shed light on the difficulties and prospects of studying food taboos in the material record.

Keywords: taboo, archaeology, archaeology of food, anthropology, zooarchaeology

© Max Price 2026

ISBNs: 9781009663571 (HB), 9781009663618 (PB), 9781009663595 (OC)
ISSNs: 2754-2971 (online), 2754-2963 (print)

Contents

1 Introduction — 1

2 A History of Anthropological Interest in Taboo — 3

3 How to Think About Taboos — 16

4 Meat Is Good to Taboo — 26

5 Food Taboos in Archaeology — 29

6 Case Studies — 38

7 Conclusion — 57

References — 61

1 Introduction

"What is the strangest thing you've eaten?" It's a question I've been asked before in many places. But at this particular moment, I was sitting in the courtyard of a concrete house in Wadi Rum, Jordan, resting after a day of excavating a small and ultimately not very productive archaeological site. The interlocutor was my Jordanian co-director, and beside me was the mapping specialist, also Jordanian, and an American undergraduate student. We were preparing to roast a lizard, *dhub* in Arabic, whose head our driver had positively blown off with an AK-47 earlier that day. Being a group of Americans and city-slicker Ammanis, none of us had a lot of experience eating reptiles. We were all intrigued and wanted to compare notes before digging in.

I'd eaten a guinea pig in Peru. The mapping specialist had eaten camel. The American student shrugged. His father had encouraged an eclectic diet. "I've eaten cat, squirrel, snake," he listed, "And raccoon." We all nodded, satisfied with the menagerie we'd collectively consumed. Someone placed the *dhub*, wrapped in tinfoil, onto the coals. "Oh," said the student "and dog."

"Ach!" cried my co-director. He looked at the student askance. "A dog?! I can understand a cat. But a dog is disgusting!" He shook his head and poked at the *dhub*. It would eventually taste like dry, gamey fish.

I've thought about this moment as I've become more interested in the anthropological phenomenon of taboos and the quest to detect and understand them in the archaeological record. To many, it may seem ironic that the thought of eating dog elicited so much disgust at the moment we were to eat lizard. In telling this story, I often ask my students to consider what food, for them, would provoke a similar reaction. Answers have included rats, insects, and humans. I try to understand how similar sentiments may have shaped the foodways, lives, and even the cultural trajectories of people in the past.

The episode in Wadi Rum reveals a social fact that turns out to be universal (or as close to it as anything is): Meat has a tendency to seem strange. In naming the "strangest" foods we'd eaten, all of us named an animal. I've eaten durian and "magic mushroom" and berries bursting with mouth-everting tannins that a book promised were edible. As a child, I once ate iron filings I'd collected from the ground with a magnet. But it's the lizards and the guinea pigs that provoke the loudest gasps.

Objectively, meat is not very strange. "With a few exceptions, (for example, pufferfish), fresh animal flesh produces no psychoactive or poisonous effects." Meat is tame when placed alongside fungi and plants such as coffee, tobacco, cannabis, *Amanita*, alcoholic drinks, mescaline-yielding cacti, ephedra, psilocybin, belladonna, and coca (some of these plant/fungal products are objects of taboos, admittedly). Unless spoiled, tainted, or undercooked, meat is rarely dangerous. As a food, the taste of meat, umami, is universally craved, and meat in its various preparations comes brimming with various flavors (e.g., "gamey," "earthy," "mild"). But it hardly compares to the universe of tastes and flavors provided by compounds in plants: sugar, cinnamon, nutmeg, chili pepper, and anise.

Why, then, does meat seem so strange?

Because meat is powerful. It possesses associations of masculinity and sexuality – meat is carnal. It is often craved in a manner unlike that of other foods except sugar and those with psychoactive and addictive effects (e.g., tobacco, coffee, or alcohol). But meat is also dangerous. It conjures up images of violence; it reminds us of death. It does not take the anthropologist long to discover that food taboos, while they can apply to various substances (e.g., alcohol to Muslims, coffee to Mormons, or, as I argue in Section 4, illicit drugs and tobacco to some Americans), *by and large*, apply to the flesh of animals. Culturally, meat *is* strange. It is weird. It is potent. It is death. It is good to taboo.

This Element will explore the archaeology of food taboos, mostly via the application of zooarchaeology and related fields to taboos on meat. Of course, there are and were food taboos on non-animal products. But meat holds the prime position. Moreover, animal bones are a commonly collected category of archaeological remains. Simply put, meat means a lot and we have a lot of evidence for it in the past. This does not imply that the archaeology of food taboos is a straightforward endeavor. The methodological difficulties of detecting taboos, not to mention understanding their social and cultural significance, represent a significant challenge.

"Archaeology is anthropology or it is nothing" (Willey and Phillips, 1958, p. 2). In order to approach taboos in the archaeological record, we must lay the anthropological groundwork. Anthropologists and other social scientists have long sought to understand taboos. That history is the subject of Section 2. In it, I include, though do not endorse, many different perspectives. In addition to jettisoning the overtly racist 19th-century frameworks, I am particularly critical of overly functionalist interpretations of taboos that construe food restrictions as biologically or ecologically adaptive. Taboos, in the final analysis, stem from what Dan Sperber (1997) has called "intuitive beliefs" and rely on magical (or associative) – and not rational – thinking. Even if they sometimes keep people from consuming harmful substances or engaging in dangerous behaviors, taboos are not arrived at through logical deductions from first principles.

Section 3 approaches a definition of taboo. The anthropological category "taboo" and the more popular uses of the term encompass a wide range of avoidance behaviors. Definitions are limiting, but they stake out the intellectual terrain and provide a compass for exploring it. They are a necessary first step in any honest analytical process.

Section 4 is a short section devoted to a key question: Why is meat so good to taboo?

Section 5 focuses on methodological problems concerning how food taboos are materialized and detected archaeologically: Who follows food taboos, what gets tabooed, and what are the physical manifestations of taboo? Politis and Saunders' (2002) ethnoarchaeological study of food taboos among Nukak communities in the Amazon makes it clear that contextual and depositional factors can severely complicate the archaeology of taboos. Fowles (2008) has pointed out that detecting taboos in archaeology relies on the absence of evidence serving as evidence of absence – an analytical process we typically train ourselves to avoid.

Section 6 examines case studies from around the globe. It becomes clear that an archaeology of taboo is much more powerful in historical settings when we can approach the topic with the combination of archaeological and textual evidence. An archaeology of food taboos is more compelling when one can approach it *deductively* – that is, with a known or hypothetical taboo – rather than *inductively* – when one is searching for "conspicuous absences" (Fowles, 2008). But this does not mean we should abandon inductive approaches. Even though we are on shakier ground, it is a worthwhile pursuit. Food taboos have been and remain an essential feature of the human condition. Writing them out of the past presents a false narrative. Yet, to include them in the tapestry, we may have to embrace informed speculation, something that the more analytically inclined archaeologists are wont to abjure.

In Section 7, I summarize the preceding sections and present some thoughts on how we can build a better analytical framework for approaching taboos in the past.

2 A History of Anthropological Interest in Taboo

Early Theories of Taboos

The word "taboo" is found across the Polynesian language family. It entered English following the publication of the journals and memoirs of crewmembers aboard James Cook voyaged all over the Pacific (1768–1780), in particular the widely read *A Voyage to the Pacific Ocean* (King, 1785), written by James King, who ultimately took command of the third voyage after Cook's death (Figure 1). These accounts detailed how Cook and his men first learned about taboos (or *tapu, kapu, tabu*, depending on the language and sometimes its transliterator).

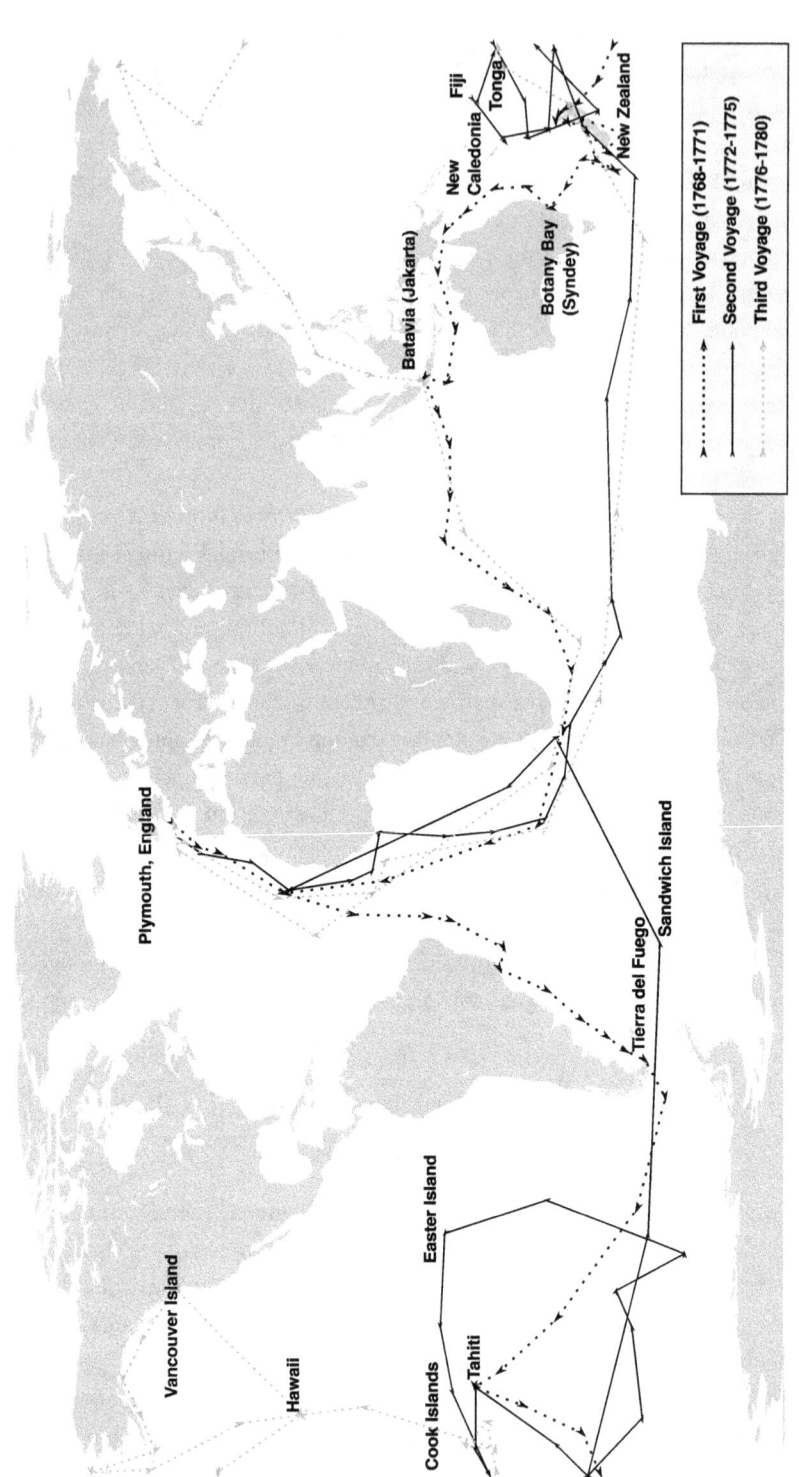

Figure 1 Cook's voyages to the Pacific. Figure by author.

> Mention hath been already made, that women are always *tabooed*, or forbidden to eat certain kind of meats. We also frequently saw several at their meals, who had the meat put into their mouths by others; and on our asking the reason of this singularity, were told, that they were tabooed, or forbidden, feed themselves. This prohibition, we understood, was always laid on them, after they had assisted at any funeral or touched a dead body, and also on other occasions. It is necessary to observe, that, on these occasions, they apply the word taboo indifferently both to persons and things. Thus they say, the natives were tabooed, or the bay was tabooed, and so of the rest. This word is also used to express any thing sacred, or eminent, or devoted. Thus the king of Owhyhee [Hawaii] was called *Eree-taboo*; a human victim, *tangata-taboo* ; and, in the same manner, among the Friendly Islanders, Tonga, the island where the king resides, is named *Tonga-taboo*. (King, 1785, p. 164)

The scrupulosity with which taboos were obeyed impressed Cook's crew, as did the punishments meted out for their transgression, which was often death (e.g., King, 1785, p. 10).

The increased activity by Euro-American mariners in the Pacific in the 19th century exposed more Western sailors to the concept of taboos, which continued to mystify them. In *Typee* (1893 [1846]), Herman Melville's (exaggerated) account of his experience among the eponymous people on the island Kuna Hiva in the Marquesas Islands, the American author reflected:

> [I]n all [Polynesian islands] exists the mysterious "Taboo," restricted in its uses to a greater or less [sic] extent. So strange and complex in its arrangements is this remarkable system, that I have in several cases met with individuals who, after residing for years among the islands of the Pacific, and acquiring a considerable knowledge of the language, have nevertheless been altogether unable to give any satisfactory account of its operations. Situated as I was in the Typee valley, I perceived every hour the effects of this all-controlling power, without in the least comprehending it. Those effects were, indeed, wide-spread and universal, pervading the most important as well as the minutest transactions of life. The savage, in short, lives in the continual observance of its dictates, which guide and control every action of his being.
> For several days after entering the valley I had been saluted at least fifty times in the twenty-four hours with the talismanic word "Taboo" shrieked in my ears, at some gross violation of its provisions, of which I had unconsciously been guilty. (Melville, 1893, p. 244)

Several pages later, Melville noted: "The word itself (taboo) is used in more than one signification. It is sometimes used by a parent to his child, when in the exercise of parental authority he forbids it to perform a particular action. Anything opposed to the ordinary customs of the islanders, although not expressly prohibited, is said to be 'taboo.'" (Melville, 1893, p. 248)

Like Melville, many travelers and travelogue readers understood taboo as an example of the superstitious ways of non-Christian peoples. Contact with and exploitation of Indigenous peoples around the globe exposed Europeans, through the distorting lens of colonialism, to practices and beliefs that appeared utterly alien. Bewitched by the ethnocentrism of the era, colonial authorities and educated Westerners, like Melville, typically saw taboos as yet more proof of the backwardness of the people they had conquered, for there are few things that seem as irrational, absurd, and ridiculous as a taboo to an outsider.

However, a few Westerners realized they had seen something similar to the Polynesian taboo closer to home. In what can be called a moment of anthropological insight, William Anderson, who had joined Cook's expedition as the *Resolution*'s surgeon and naturalist, wrote in his notebook on July 11, 1777: "There is another custom amongst them call'd Taboo whose precise meaning we do not well understand. The word itself implies no more than a thing is not to be touch'd … In some cases it appears to resemble the Levitical law of purification" (Beaglehole, 1967, pp. 947–948).

In fact, it became apparent that taboos were quite pervasive in European cultures, even if, prior to Cook's voyages, English had no word for a type of ritual prohibition enforced by emotional response. Though it took time for them to admit it, English and later other Europeans had intimate experience with taboos, and not just in the food laws of the Hebrew Bible obeyed by Jews. It would not be long before "taboo" entered common usage to indicate something strictly and/or irrationally proscribed. For example, Edmund Burke used the term to defend himself against his colleague, Charles James Fox, who had criticized Burke's *Reflections on the Revolution in France* (Burke, 2015 [1791]). In his *An Appeal from the New to the Old Whigs*, Burke complained, in the third person, "the topic of France is tabooed or forbidden ground to Mr. Burke, and to Mr. Burke alone" (Burke, 2015, p. 387). Three decades later, in 1822, the poet Robert Southey began a letter to his eighteen-year-old daughter: "Fortune, I think, has fitted you with a physician to your liking. He has *tabooed* ham, vinegar, red-herrings, and all fruits" (Warter, 1856, p. 305).

The concept of taboo gained more popular usage and attracted academic attention in the Victorian period. Steiner (1956, p. 50) postulates that this interest in taboos reflected the twofold nature of bourgeois society of the period: On the one hand, it had adopted a "rationalist approach to religion" that demanded scepticism of beliefs. On the other, it held fast to numerous taboos, especially surrounding sexuality; this was a time when museums attached fig leaves to Greek statues and polite society referred to pants as "unmentionables."

All the while, European imperialism continued apace. Contact with distant cultures and their belief systems (and the suppression of them) had become commonplace.

Anthropology and other social sciences cut their teeth in this age defined by colonial expansion and cultural self-critique. Early anthropologists found in the concept of taboo something that was characteristic of both the "primitive" and the "civilized." It was also, as Anderson recognized during his voyages with Cook, a conspicuous feature of the foodways of the great internal European other: Jews. It is perhaps unsurprising that many of the foundational social theorists of taboo were either wayward Protestants inclined to religious critique (Smith, Frazer) or secular Jews (Freud, Durkheim, Lévy-Bruhl).

James Frazer's article "Taboo" in the ninth edition of the *Encyclopaedia Britannica* (Frazer, 1886) is as good a point as any to mark the beginning of social scientific scholarship on taboo. Frazer saw taboos as a primitive type of religious thought, an early step on the road to enlightenment that ran from superstition to religion to rational thought. Frazer recognized that taboos existed in the "enlightened" cultures of antiquity and modernity. He came to realize that taboos were a universal cultural phenomenon (Steiner, 1956, p. 97), even though he understood them as primitive holdovers: "Thus on the taboo were grafted the golden fruits of law and morality, while the parent stem dwindled slowly into the sour crabs and empty husks of popular superstition on which the swine of modern society are still content to feed." (Frazer, 1886, p. 17)

Frazer continued his work on taboo in the third volume of his tome *The Golden Bough* (Frazer, 1911). In it, he sketched a historiographical framework composed of three eras: magic/superstition, religion (as in supplication to anthropomorphized deities), and science. Frazer argued that magic, religion, and science each attempt to cause physical changes in the world through specific actions, be they spells, prayers, or chemistry. Each era was a response to the failures of the previous one to effect change in the world. Taboos belonged to the era of magic, and Frazer essentially saw taboos as negative magic. Both taboo and (positive) magic involve "the misapplication of the association of ideas by similarity and contiguity" (Steiner, 1956, p. 100).[1]

Robertson Smith was a close colleague of Frazer. Like Frazer, he recognized the similarity between Polynesian taboos and Levitical food laws. But Smith

---

[1] This idea was later critiqued by Marett (1909), who claimed that it was better to understand taboo as negative *mana* (or spiritual power), not magic in the sense that Frazer saw it (Steiner, 1956, pp. 101–111).

went further, perceiving within the concept of taboo the key to understanding the nature of "the holy" in ancient Israelite and later Abrahamic religion. He articulated his thesis in his magnum opus, *The Religion of the Semites* (Smith, 2017 [1894]), a book whose critical approach and insistence on a multi-authored Pentateuch earned him a trial for heresy in the Free Church of Scotland (Steiner, 1956, p. 55). Smith believed that the Levitical concept of holiness and the prohibitions surrounding it related to animistic beliefs. He saw the perpetuation of such taboos in modern-day Judaism and Islam as essentially vestigial superstitions in religions that had evolved past them. To Smith, taboos had no place in an enlightened theology (Steiner, 1956, pp. 53–58).

Émile Durkheim's *Elementary Forms of Religious Life* (1995 [1912]), based on ethnographic work conducted by others in Australia, centers on a hypothetical dichotomy between the "sacred" and "profane." The "sacred" was the essential feature of religion and taboos, at least initially, served the all-important role of keeping the two separate (Durkheim, 1995, p. 306). Thus,

> The consumption of food brings about an especially intimate form of contact. Thence arises the prohibition against eating sacred animals or plants, especially those serving as the totem. ... This prohibition has sometimes been explained in terms of the mythical kinship that unites man with the animals whose name he bears – the animals being protected, presumably, by the sympathy they inspire, as kin. That the origin of this prohibition is not simply revulsion caused by the sense of familial solidarity is brought about by the following: Consumption of the forbidden flesh is presumed to cause sickness and death automatically. Thus, forces of a different sort have come into play – forces analogous to those forces in all religions that are presumed to react against sacrilege.
>
> Further, while certain foods, because sacred, are forbidden to the profane, other foods, because profane, are forbidden to persons endowed with special sacredness. (Durkheim, 1995, pp. 307–308)

In this passage, Durkheim also attended to the ambivalence that often surrounds taboos, an idea that had also figured prominently in the work of Frazer and Smith. Taboos apply to things that inspire awe/worship and disgust. These sentiments, though seemingly in opposition, are in fact two sides of the same coin. Thus, something that is taboo is dangerous, but it can also serve as medicine (Durkheim, 1995, p. 411).

Wilhelm Wundt (1921 [1916]) rejected the notion that taboos protected the "sacred. His argument rested upon the claim that so-called "primitive" religions do not distinguish between the sacred and unclean, and therefore do not possess a concept of the sacred at all." Wundt argued that taboos stemmed from a fear of "demonic" (not sacred) forces. He then dwelt upon the connection between the totem and the taboo, arguing that taboos began with prohibitions on eating the meat of a totem animal. That the Polynesian and many other cases of taboo did not involve totemic animals was not a problem for Wundt; these societies had simply evolved to the point where they could apply taboos more broadly.

Wundt's work was absorbed by Sigmund Freud, who differentiated taboo from moral and other types of prohibition, and placed the origins of taboo in associative feelings, not the logical working from first principles. Like Wundt before him, Freud saw taboo as rooted in dread and fear. Freud's work, especially *Totem and Taboo* (Freud, 2020 [1913]), stands out not because of its particular insights into the anthropological phenomenon of taboo (he largely followed Wundt, Frazer, and Durkheim), but because of his drawing of connections to his patients exhibiting "obsessional neuroses," or what we would nowadays refer to as obsessive compulsive disorder (OCD). Freud went so far as to suggest that OCD could be referred to as a "taboo disease" (Freud, 2020, p. 23). After all, taboos and obsessions lack a clear motive, follow their own "internal necessity" rather than logic, are often marked by contagion, and give rise to rituals (Steiner, 1956, p. 135).

Freud made several blunders, anthropological and psychological. He forwarded the demonstrably false notion that the singular worry of the "obsessional neurotic" is that harm will come upon their friends or family if they do not perform their rituals, and he asserted that so-called "primitive peoples" or "savages" had childlike minds. For Freud, only the allegedly more enlightened cognition of Europeans could properly distinguish between a religious notion of the "sacred" and a more physical or health-related notion of the "unclean." Indeed, the repression of unconscious desires in "civilized" Europeans was a leading cause of distress, he claimed.

Freud got a lot wrong, but he made an important connection between social and psychological fears. We can rescue some of his thesis. Particularly apt was Freud's observation that many fears are confronted with and contained through specific actions – rituals – whose symbolic power derives from what is often "associative" or "magical" thinking.

Associative thinking involves making connections between categories that are not necessarily related. This can foster more rapid cognitive movement compared to rational thought, which operates in a logical manner from first principles (Beaty and Kenett, 2023). Magical thinking dovetails with associative thinking, but stems ultimately from the human drive to determine causality (Rosengren and French, 2013). It involves attributing intentionality or animate qualities to the inanimate world as well as the belief that one's thoughts and actions can affect the world through processes that are not physically observable (Piaget, 1930, pp. 131–162; Rosengren and French, 2013). Magical thinking thus involves the imagination of causal relations, often attributable to ethereal forces, between categories connected by associative thinking. While magical thinking may peak in early childhood, as the psychologist Jean Piaget observed long ago, it remains a feature of human cognition into adulthood and is connected to the human impulse to imagine (Rosengren and French, 2013, p. 43). Praying to a deity to intercede in the world, obeying a taboo to prevent illness, cursing an enemy, wearing lucky socks to a sporting event, blaming one's misfortune on witchcraft, and feeling guilt when a person one resented dies suddenly are all examples of magical thinking.

Freud was essentially correct that these types of cognition underlie taboos and often play a key role in OCD, though he was wrong to label of associative and magical thinking "primitive." It barely needs mentioning that even self-described "rational" (and neurotypical) people act on irrational fears (Rozin, Markwith, and Ross, 1990; Nemeroff and Rozin, 1992; Rozin, Markwith, and Nemeroff, 1992).

Taboo in Early Mid 20th Century Anthropology

Twentieth century anthropology built upon the early works concerning taboo, but injected into them a dose of cultural relativism that, thankfully, neutralized most of the racist and ethnocentric aspects of such theories. While virtually every major anthropologist has had their say on the topic of taboo, we only have space to review a few.

A. R. Radcliffe-Brown, the father of structural functionalism, viewed society as a rather harmonious collection of mutually supporting structures. He framed his approach to taboos in this vein, but more specifically with reference to the philosopher Ralph Barton Perry's work, *General Theory of Value* (1926). Perry and Radcliffe-Brown conceptualized value as occurring when a subject has "interest" in an object (Radcliffe-Brown, 1939, p. 19). A society can be understood as a "system of values" (Radcliffe-Brown, 1939, p. 20) in which there is "harmonization" of individuals' interests and an agreement concerning shared "social values" (Radcliffe-Brown, 1939, pp. 20–22). Social values benefit individuals, but they also promote social cohesion. Cooking and eating, for example, are valuable to each individual by providing calories, but food also brings people together and confers meaning. For Radcliffe-Brown, taboos not only mark things of social value, they also *make* value. In other words, they not only protect, they also provide structure. On the other hand, while taboos offer a sense of protection from things that appear dangerous, they also create anxiety around those things – thus making them appear dangerous in the first place and thereby erecting boundaries on social behavior (Radcliffe-Brown, 1939, p. 39).

Margaret Mead (1937) took a somewhat different, if still structuralist, path to taboo. She stressed the Polynesian origin of the term "taboo," but argued that if it were to have an anthropological significance, the concept had to be separated from its original context (Mead, 1937, pp. 503–504). She offered the following definition: "a negative sanction ... against participation in any situation of such inherent danger that the very act of participation will recoil upon the violator" (Mead, 1937, p. 502). Decades later, Mead (1978) considered the possibility of harnessing the power of taboos for social good. Writing for the women's magazine *Redbook*, she argued that the best way to prevent sexual harassment in the workplace was to develop a taboo on such relations, similar to the incest taboo. One could argue that, with the increased attention to sexual harassment and inappropriate workplace relationships in the wake of the #MeToo movement, such a taboo is starting to emerge.

By the middle of the 20th century, anthropology had produced a sizable volume of theory on taboos, their meanings, and their origins. Playing the role of grand synthesizer, Franz Steiner in his lectures on taboo, carefully compiled for publication by Laura Bohannan and with a preface by E. E. Evans-Pritchard (Steiner, 1956), offered one of the most thorough evaluations of the concept of taboo. The slim book, which remains as enlightening as it was seventy years ago, reviewed the writings of Robertson Smith, James Frazer, Margaret Mead, R. R. Marret, Sigmund Freud, Arnold Van Gennep, Wilhelm Wundt, and A. R. Radcliffe-Brown. Steiner's prose is biting, his critique unrelenting. Not even Radcliffe-Brown, Steiner's teacher, escaped unscathed.

Yet for all his criticism, Steiner appears hesitant, even equivocal, in proposing a definition:

> Taboo is concerned (1) with all the social mechanisms of obedience which have ritual significance; (2) with specific and restrictive behavior in dangerous situations ... (3) with the protection of individuals who are in danger, and (4) with the protection of society from those endangered – and therefore dangerous – person ... Taboo is an element of all those situations in which attitudes to values are expressed in terms of danger behaviour. (Steiner, 1956, pp. 20–21)

Steiner concludes that a taboo "gives notice that danger lies not in the whole situation, but only in certain specified actions concerning it" (Steiner, 1956, pp. 146–147). In other words, taboos allow one to focus on certain dangers – and ritually keep them at bay through avoidance – in a chaotic and unknowable world.

Symbolic and Functionalist Explanations

From the 1960s onward, two strands of taboo theories developed: symbolic and functional. The first was broadly consistent with interpretations of taboo proffered by previous generations. Victor Turner (1964) extended Van Gennep's (1960) *Rites de Passage* [originally 1909], identifying taboos as protective of liminal spaces, people, or things. The categorical uncertainty of the betwixt-and-between makes it dangerous. Like the sacred in Durkheim, that liminality must be separated from the everyday world; taboos serve that purpose. In a similar vein, Mary Douglas (1966) conceived of taboos as enforcing purity, preventing allegedly dangerous symbolic mixtures. Her canonical example was the Leviticus taboos and their justifications (e.g., the pig with its cloven hooves but lack of rumination), although she later recanted this theory (Douglas, 1975, pp. 276–318, 2002, p. viii).

Perhaps the most significant of the symbolic interpretations remains that of Claude Lévi-Strauss. *The Elementary Forms of Kinship* (1969) focused on the incest taboo, but its insights are more broadly applicable. Reading Freud (2020), Lévi-Strauss agreed that the incest taboo was a critical and universal feature of human existence, but Lévi-Strauss rejected the notion that it derived from innate (psychologically derived) sexual desires between related individuals. He argued the incest taboo was a social, not psychological, milestone in human existence that laid the foundations for kinship systems and, thereby, culture. It represented a sort of Rubicon in human evolution over which culture passed in pursuit of its goal of subordinating nature. The incest taboo made us human because it forced non-related individuals to form social units as families became socially interdependent for the exchange of marriage partners (women, for Lévi-Strauss). This reproductive interdependence precipitated other material and non-material forms of exchange and interaction. This "alliance theory" holds that the basis of human social existence is the exchange of women between families. "The incest prohibition is at once on the threshold of culture, in culture, and in one sense . . . culture itself" (Lévi-Strauss, 1969, p. 12).

More recently, Maurice Godelier has modified Lévi-Strauss' argument in *The Metamorphoses of Kinship* (2011). Critiquing the notion that marriage exchange and the incest taboo represent the original basis of human social organization (Godelier, 2011, p. 381), Godelier nonetheless argues that the incest taboo, though not entirely universal (e.g., brother-sister marriage in Persian and Egyptian history), reflects a universal concern with controlling sexuality, which can be dangerous to society. Society needs rules (such as taboos) to hem in sexual desire. In turn, these rules give shape to human society – as Lévi-Strauss argued, they are culture itself, in a sense – but they also protect society *in the process of its reproduction*. I will take this idea further in my own explanation of taboos.

One of the most important ethnographic works in the past few decades is Valerio Valeri's posthumous book, *The Forest of Taboos*. Valeri provides an updated synthesis of theories of the taboo, with a particular emphasis on the French social anthropological literature (Valeri, 2000, pp. 43–113). Especially when read in conjunction with Steiner, Valeri exposes the reader to the full breadth of 100+ years of scholarship, offering trenchant commentary. Mostly, however, *The Forest of Taboos* is based on ethnographic work with Huaulu communities in the Moluku Islands, a people who possess many taboos (*maquwoli* in the local language). Many pertain to food and hunting.

Valeri's theory of taboo is Durkheimian: Taboos serve to keep things at an appropriate ontological distance from people – things too dissimilar or too similar are avoided. "The number and importance of food taboos reflect the exceptional dangerousness that Huaulu thought attributes to digestion, a dangerousness ultimately due to the fact that eating amounts to reconstituting oneself by assimilating others – that one is what one eats and that what one eats is not, ontologically speaking, radically different from what one is." (Valeri, 2000, p. 162)

Valeri thus builds his theory on the assumption that taboos have something to do with the self, with the negotiation between subject and object, and the differentiation, which is to say identification, of a person in a cultural and natural world.

Yet, Valeri is careful not to argue that taboos simply keep the self at a distance, or prevent the accumulation of too many identical things, thus differentiating his theory from those of Françoise Héritier (1979) and Alain Testart (1991). Instead, he strives to build upon the theory of Alfred Gell (1979), who saw taboos as constructive of the self by allowing a person to separate themselves bodily from the world with respect to three socially charged activities: killing, eating, and having sex.

Valeri recognized that hunting and eating meat is particularly fraught for the Huaulu hunter. The hunter, according to Valeri, perceives both ontological closeness to and distance from their prey. They thus feel a need to negotiate a tension between cannibalism and the ingestion of something so essentially different from the human as to risk becoming non-food. Taboos perform this negotiation. As such, according to Valeri, taboo is fundamentally derived from concerns over both morality and identity, and links the two through practices of avoidance.

All of these theories just reviewed constitute symbolic frameworks for making sense of taboos. The other strand is functionalist. There is a broad literature, but the anthropologist perhaps most identified with this approach is Marvin Harris, who, along with others, sought environmental or biological explanations for taboo. Thus, for example, one reads that pigs became taboo in

Judaism and Islam because they required too much water (Harris, 1974), that food taboos in Amazonia can be explained by "the faunal productivity" of the region (Ross, 1978, p. 15), that incest taboos are an evolutionary adaptation to prevent inbreeding (Van den Berghe, 1980), that taboos which prevent children and women from eating meat in New Guinea is an adaptation to endemic malaria (Lepowsky, 1985), and that food taboos on pregnant women in Fiji evolved to reduce the risk of fish poisoning (Henrich and Henrich, 2010). Such ideas have proved popular. They offer simple explanations for the seemingly irrational behavior of ritual avoidance. They suggest that history, social behavior, and the mind itself can yield their secrets provided one has the right "key," that everything can be explained by a simple sentence. Such simplification of the world is comforting in the same way that following a taboo is: It provides the illusion of comprehension in the unknowable chaos that defines our existence.

There are several problems with functionalist interpretations. Most have proven all too easy to shoot down on factual bases alone (Diener and Robkin, 1978; Simoons, 1994; Fessler and Navarrete, 2003; Price, 2021). But on a deeper level, one can always argue that *any* practice serves a practical purpose, just as people can (and often do) devise reasonable explanations for behavior they would otherwise deem irrational, impulsive, or immoral (Schwitzgebel and Ellis, 2017). Taboos, because they involve avoidance in a world of danger and death, can always be made to appear rational or functional.

None of this is to say that taboos cannot be functional or beneficial. It is possible that some may have helped societies or populations succeed on evolutionary timescales. But we should not conflate effect with cause. Perhaps it is useful to take a page out of Freud's book and draw an analogy to OCD. A person with OCD may have obsessions that are advantageous. Contamination OCD, with the compulsion to wash one's hands, will reduce their risk of contracting the flu. However, this benefit does not explain OCD, its causes, or the experience of people living with it. One does not have OCD because one is afraid of catching a virus; OCD causes a person to fixate on the fear of catching a virus. The same is true for taboos. Functionalist explanations offer at best partial explanations for why taboos emerge in the first place, how they persist and evolve, and how people experience abiding by them. Furthermore, just as disease avoidance can allow a person with OCD to rationalize effectively irrational thoughts and in doing so occasionally resist treatment, functionalist explanations can obfuscate, even for those who abide by taboos, the real reasons taboos develop, persist, evolve, and in some cases disappear.

Thinking about Taboos Outside Anthropology

Several important contributions to the study for taboos have come from outside anthropology. Allan and Burridge (2006), two linguists, examined tabooed words and censorship. They note that taboos often involve the body – eating, bodily excretions, death, birth, and speaking, thus connecting taboo with identity. They also provide a helpful analogy for the contagion aspect of taboo: "It is as if the tabooed object were like a radioactive fuel rod, which will have dire effects on anyone who some into direct contact with it unless they know how to protect themselves." (Allan and Burridge, 2006, p. 5)

Bridging psychology and evolutionary anthropology, Fessler and Navarrete (2003) contribute to the study of food taboos, especially those on meat. After reviewing and rejecting symbolic and functionalist theories, they develop an approach to taboos based on "normative moralization," or the way in which common behavioral traits in a population become perceived as right, and "egocentric empathy," or putting oneself in another's shoes (Fessler and Navarrete, 2003, pp. 14–15). The first creates group ideals, such as taboos; the second is responsible for emotional response to (and policing of) others' behavior. Fessler and Navarrete then tackle a question important to this Element – why is meat so good to taboo? They answer it with a combination of evolutionary psychology (meat spoils easily and can cause sickness) and the symbolic power of animals cross-culturally. We will revisit these themes in Section 4.

Fessler and Navarrete note the importance of the emotion of disgust in the psychological experience of food taboos. Much of the work on this topic has been conducted by Paul Rozin and colleagues (Rozin *et al.*, 1997; Rozin, Markwith, and Stoess, 1997; Rozin, Haidt, and McCauley, 2008). Their work has shown that disgust is a powerful emotion, one learned early in childhood, that provides "culture's most effective means to enforce a prohibition" (Rozin *et al.*, 1997, p. 79). Indeed, psychologically speaking, the power of taboos often derives from the disgust they elicit. The clinical psychologist Susan Miller (2004), a specialist in shame and disgust, refers to the latter as "the gatekeeper emotion."

Concluding Remarks

What is a taboo? In the most basic sense, taboos involve fear, but it is often a *confusing* fear, one mixed with other emotions, including disgust (Miller, 2004; Rozin, Haidt, and McCauley, 2008). A sense of awe and, in some cases, (repressed) desire is not uncommon. Frazer, Smith, and Freud all drew attention to these seemingly paradoxical emotions. The Polynesian concept of *tabu/tapu/*

kapu is also ambiguous – a tabooed thing or person can be seen as either too good or too vile to be touched.

We should also attend to the issue that taboos are implicated in identity. Mary Douglas put it succinctly in her review of Valeri's (2000) *The Forest of Taboos*: "taboos reinforce the oppositions that construct the universe. Animal-human, male-female, these oppositions shore up delicate distinctions that could easily dissolve into each other" (Douglas, 2000, p. 2288). DeBoer (1987), in his assessment of food taboos in the Amazon, reached a similar conclusion: "you are what you don't eat." Taboos negotiate in-group and out-group dynamics. Taboos are the wild beasts that howl on the borderlines, separating social identities from one another through emotionally charged avoidance behaviors.

Digging deeper, things become fuzzy. Steiner (1956, p. 141), the master synthesizer of his era, correctly noted that "taboo" is a catch-all term for many different types of prohibition practices. Indeed, each theorist's perspective on taboo is influenced by the particular cases they examine and their unique worldview. For Valeri, taboo meant the *maquwoli* of the Huaulu; for Durkheim it was the taboos he read about in ethnographies of Aboriginal Australians. Freud had in mind the "obsessional neuroses" of his patients, while Turner and Ven Gennep conjured to their minds prohibitions that applied to the ritual initiate. Douglas (and myself for that matter) approached the subject through the pig taboo in the Hebrew Bible. Meanwhile, Radcliffe-Brown and Mead fit taboos into their general structuralist understanding of culture. Taboo is, then, an anthropological abstraction, a theoretical thing that is used to understand certain prohibition behaviors through classification and analogy. But because it can be viewed in many ways, and because it comes in many forms, the issue of how to think about taboos presents different problems for the anthropologist depending on the context.

3 How to Think About Taboos

Taboo and Rationality

Are taboos rational? This is a thorny question. Perhaps a useful framework for approaching it is via Max Weber's (2019 [1921]) taxonomy of social action, with rational acts deriving from a clear and reasoned train of thought (logical deduction) based upon a set of reasonable first principles or assumptions. Among rational social actions, he distinguished between *Zweckrationalität* ("goal-ended rationality") and *Wertrationalität* ("value rationality"). *Zweckrationalität* describes actions reasoned from a practical goal "I do not eat meat because I have high cholesterol." *Wertrationalität* describes actions reasoned from a moral first principle: for example, "I do not eat meat because

I believe that animals should not be harmed." Weber counterposed these rational types to nonrational social action, notably those deriving from emotions or from tradition (Weber, 2019, p. 101). When we consider the psychology of taboos – that is, what people are thinking when they follow them or are confronted with the option of transgression – we can sometimes detect a mix of Weberian social action types. Ultimately, however, I argue that, in essence and in daily practice, taboos are nonrational.[2]

Before proceeding down this path, I want to make it clear that I am *not* making a value-judgment distinction between "high and low" cognition, as the early taboo theorists did. All human thought in every cultural setting is a mix of rational and nonrational thinking. Already mentioned, one particularly important form of nonrational cognition at play in the reproduction and daily experience of taboos is "associative thinking." This is the more fluid, pattern-seeking type of thought that, according to some psychologists, is the basis of human creativity (Mednick, 1962; Beaty and Kenett, 2023). Associative thinking can move faster and in much less predictable directions than rational step-wise reasoning from first principles, and thus plays a critical role in human cognition. If associative thinking gives us art, stories, inventions, and new experimental approaches, rational thinking allows us to philosophize, write code, analyze text, and perform mathematical proofs.

Taboos may appear to be *wertrational* in that they can, in theory, be connected to moral first principles. Anthropologists have tried to delineate these connections. For example, Lévi-Strauss (1969) argued that the force of the incest taboo derives from the gift-giving imperative. This sounds nice as a theory, but the reality is that the connections between the ideological values that a community holds (e.g., gift-giving) and the taboos it follows (incest avoidance) are almost always vague, tenuous, or variable between individuals. At best, taboos can be said to represent an unconscious manifestation of structure. Yet the fact remains that taboos, as they are experienced, are felt and followed, not reasoned from first principles.

Similarly, taboos may appear *zweckrational*, especially if they prevent illness (Henrich and Henrich, 2010) or are environmentally adaptive (Harris, 1974). This line of reasoning is the basis of the functionalist approach to taboos. However, *Zweckrationalität* is not about whether an action leads to a positive outcome; it is about whether it was reasoned from explicit recognition of that outcome. While it may prevent the accumulation of deleterious mutations, the

---

[2] The dichotomy between associative and rational thought is an oversimplification – perhaps a repackaging of Descartes (Papineau and Heyes, 2006). Within the categories, there is much variation; for example, goal-directed associations versus free-association (Beaty and Kenett, 2023). These cautions notwithstanding, the dichotomy is useful as a heuristic.

incest taboo is not *zweckrational*. The reason close relatives avoid sexual contact is not that they have calculated the odds of genetic anomalies in their potential offspring, but because they are fundamentally repulsed by the idea of it. Were it simply *zweckrational*, nonreproductive sex between close relatives would not be taboo.

There are, of course, *wertrational* and *zweckrational* forms of avoidance: moral and health-related vegetarianism, for example, or practicing safe sex to avoid contracting an STD. But these are *not*, I argue, taboos, though they can give rise to taboos, or feed into the emotional content of a taboo. To be taboo, the sentiments surrounding avoidance behavior must include an emotional response eclipsing, or even fully replacing, rational thought. For what gives a taboo meaning is its connection to moral rectitude through the medium of associational thinking. What gives a taboo power is the emotion of disgust (Rozin et al., 1997; Miller, 2004).

Another way of approaching this issue is through Dan Sperber's (1997) dichotomy between *intuitive beliefs* and *reflective beliefs*. Intuitive beliefs are those that are felt, that are not questioned, that appear as "spontaneous inference" (Sperber, 1997, p. 79). They arise from received traditions and associative thinking. They guide behavior without requiring self-conscious questioning. Reflective beliefs, on the other hand, are more open to scrutiny. They derive from observations. Such beliefs may be incorrect (one can reflectively believe the sun goes round the earth), but their explanations can be articulated in a clear and step-by-step fashion (the sun appears to traverse the sky, ergo it revolves around the earth).

Taboos derive from intuitive beliefs. They rely on associational thinking. They are therefore fundamentally nonrational.

One could object that, while taboos may derive from intuitive beliefs, people follow them for all sorts of reasons, some of which are rational. On the Cook expedition, for example, women avoided a tabooed sweet potato field claiming they would be killed by their king if they trespassed (Steiner, 1956, p. 25). The simple desire to avoid this type of punishment would be a *zweckrational* reason for steering clear of sweet potato fields. Similarly, some Jews claim to avoid pork for reasons that could be considered *wertrational*: They abstain from it to belong to their community, to enact their Jewish identity.

Rationality may therefore play a role in preventing transgression. However, I would argue that if rationality becomes dominant, if *Zweck-* or *Wertrationalität* overshadows its emotional content, a taboo is not long for this world. In becoming an object of rationality, taboo strays into the realm of reflective beliefs, opening it up to scrutiny and challenge. This is a key issue for any archaeology of taboos, which by necessity takes a long-term perspective.

Things become a bit more complicated when we consider effects that are believed to occur. Valeri's Huaulu informants cited a number of specific negative outcomes to taboo violation: for example, developing yaws on one's buttocks if one told a sacred story during the daytime; losing one's teeth if one ate marsupial meat with lime or chili; blindness if one came into contact with a menstruating woman (Valeri, 2000, p. 150). Similarly, in the United States, once-popular "urban myths" stipulated that masturbation could cause blindness, hairy palms, or infertility. And if TV and movies tell us anything, Americans seem willing to believe that eating human flesh causes prion-based neurological illnesses. This belief, drawn from the association of *kuru* disease with mortuary endocannibalism among the Fore (Rhodes, 1997), stems from a mistaken understanding of the mechanism of prion disease transmission within a population[3] (examples include the films *The Book of Eli* and *We Are What We Are*, as well as *The X-Files* episode "Our Town"). One could argue that, while the initial premise may derive from an empirical error, within the particular cultural context, it is *zweckrational* to follow such taboos.

Again, I would argue that, if tracked closely, the logic of illness or other specific misfortune following from taboo violation is, in the final analysis, associative rather than rational, intuitive rather than reflective. The "logic" underpinning the illnesses or physical consequences usually betrays some analogical connection to the violating act. Discussing how his Huaulu informants believed that eating tabooed meat would cause skin diseases, Valeri (2000, pp. 144–145) contends the diseases bear a resemblance to the skin of certain animals, that the diseases "eats" the skin in the same way the person ate the meat, and that the very visible nature of skin disease matches the social nature of eating. The fear of blindness among would-be American onanists references the visual stimulus of the masturbatory act, the hairy palms a reversion to an animal state, and infertility its non-procreative nature. The fear of *kuru*-like disease, with its uncontrollable shaking and laughing, elides neatly with a fear of loss of self-control that we are willing to believe accompanies cannibalism.

Another reason to be skeptical that rationality underlies taboos is that, in many cases, the consequences of transgression are ill-defined. Undergraduate students I've spoken with do not know what would happen if they ate a dog other than "feeling bad." Others identify a nebulous sense of "bad luck" as the consequence of taboo violation. This cannot be rational. Because the specific

---

[3] Eating any type of meat, especially neural tissue, carries the risk of contracting a prion-based illness. The reason *kuru* was common among Fore women who ate their dead was that randomly occurring prions were allowed to recirculate into the population, and thereby accumulate. There is nothing particularly risky, per se, about cannibalism other than that it closes the loop of the foodchain.

outcome is unknown, there does not exist a logical connection between cause (taboo violation) and effect ("*something* bad will happen").

On the flip side, this general feeling of bad luck makes taboo violation a ready-made *explanation* for any misfortune that may befall a person. Life is full of miseries; and one can never be *certain* one did not trigger one by accidentally violating a taboo– or that someone close to them did. Thus, one of Politis' Nukak informants blamed her epilepsy on her mother bathing her in an area tainted by the feces of tapirs, the most powerful of the animals in the Nukak cosmology (Politis, 2007, pp. 295–296). Such thinking is part of an arguably natural human desire to make sense of a chaotic world and to live under the illusion that bad things do not happen to good people. "If suffering can be related to taboo, then, it ceases to be senseless" (Valeri, 2000, p. 149). In this sense, the nebulous consequences of taboo violation offer a certain type of reassurance that the world still makes sense, that morality is meaningful in a physical way. This is a positive spin. The negative one is that people can chalk up another's suffering to presumed sins or transgressions – "victim blaming." Not only is this unfair, but it also may discourage helping society's most vulnerable. Similarly, people with illnesses that become subject to taboos, whether Hansen's Disease or HIV/AIDS, also suffer social stigma. There may be a tendency to blame their illness on moral turpitude.

A final issue pertains to variation in taboo following within a cultural setting and over time. People may follow a taboo for different reasons. A visitor, for example, may abide by a taboo out of respect for their hosts (*wertrational*); a skeptic might do so only out of fear of punishment (*zweckrational*). Though I admit I am getting close to splitting hairs, these cases reflect rule-following more than subscribing to a taboo, since there is no emotion surrounding the taboo itself. But even among those who subscribe to the taboo, there will be variation in how those emotions are felt and understood. There may be particular variation over time. It is essential that we differentiate the sentiments that give rise to the initial origin/development of a taboo from the way in which it is put into action and thought about at a later period (Steiner, 1956; Altmann, Angelini, and Spiciarich, 2020, pp. 3–4; Price, 2021, p. 114). And as easily as a taboo can "decay" into a *wert-* or *zweckrational* rule, it is also possible to imagine how a rationally conceived law (e.g., a sumptuary law intended to restrict a type of food to the elite) can evolve into a taboo if the original rationale was forgotten.

There is a difference between the "function" a taboo might have in a society, the rules it imposes upon people, and the psychological motivations that underpin it. A taboo can serve a "rational" purpose, such as preventing contagion, and people may follow it out of simple fear of retribution. But the substance of taboo relies on magical thinking, explanations for which are often tautological ("it is bad to touch the statue because touching the statue is bad") or based upon a false premise ("if I eat pork, I will get leprosy"). In the latter case, were the premise shown to be incorrect ("pork cannot cause leprosy") the injunction would remain, replaced either by another explanation that fits the received wisdom and common sense of the day ("pork can cause trichinosis") or a nonspecific sense of foreboding ("I still feel it is wrong"). If rationality breaks through, the taboo evaporates into a reflective belief or the avoidance behavior disappears altogether.

None of this is to say that taboos are meaningless or arbitrary. One can understand why people harbor certain taboos and, in doing so, reveal aspects of their culture. Taboos on eating dog in Western culture, for example, are connected to the place of that animal in the home and the family: Cynophagy is tantamount to cannibalism. Taboos among the Nukak concentrate on large animals, including deer, anteater, and especially the tapir, which are understood to be "like people." In the Nukak cosmology, such animals embody ancestors' *yorehat* (one of the several types of spiritual forces that reside within a living person). Killing and eating these animals is synonymous with killing and eating the ancestors (Politis, 2007, p. 295). Taboos, then, offer powerful statements about who we are by defining what we will not do (at least in theory). For that reason, taboos are at the core of social identity. They reproduce social categories such as age, gender, ethnicity; in turn, taboos are reproduced by these categories (Simoons, 1961; DeBoer, 1987; Price, 2021).

How Taboos Work

People avoid many things for many reasons. Pregnancy can cause a strong disgust for certain foods. Animals or people with terminal-stage rabies exhibit an uncontrollable aversion to water (hydrophobia). People with OCD often avoid situations, objects, or people who seem to them a source of contamination. People suffering from specific phobia (SP) have idiosyncratic fears. Some of these are common enough to warrant naming: arachnophobia (fear of spiders), agoraphobia (fear of the outside or crowds), or even turophobia (fear of cheese). Some foods disgust us individually; I personally cannot stand the taste of goat cheese. Anyone who has had the unpleasant experience of food poisoning has probably experienced a temporary aversion to the foods vomited up.

Even though many of these aversions can be classified as "emotional" and involve the autonomic nervous system, none of them are taboos because they pertain to individuals, not communities. Valeri recognized this difference in recounting the story of a Huaulu man who would not eat sago, one of the main staple foods. When asked, Valeri's informants replied "*Emaquwoli ipiam*" ("he has the taboo of sago"). Valeri referred to these individual aversions as "allergies" to distinguish them from taboos (Valeri, 2000, p. 129). Use of that term would irritate an immunologist, but for the purposes of this Element, it is preferable to "taboo."

But there is a similarity between these personal aversions and taboos. Freud (2020) argued that the psychological experience of abiding by a taboo is the same as that of phobias and obsessional disorders. For Freud, the obsessive-compulsive patient was a "civilized" person succumbing to their "primitive mind." We have to reject his race-based logic and mental model, but he was not entirely off the mark in comparing the psychological manifestations of a taboo and those of phobias, obsessions, and personal aversions. In all cases, what drives the compulsion to avoid is nonrational and emotional. But scale matters. What makes a taboo different from, say, my hatred of goat cheese or the discomfort a person with OCD feels when imagining contact with a contaminated surface is that a taboo is a *social institution*. While it has a psychological manifestation, it exists beyond the scale of the individual. This is precisely why taboos are so heavily implicated in ethnicity and other forms of social identity.

One can thus draw the following diagram:

Figure 2 shows qualitative differences, but the lines between them are not always clear. One cannot say precisely how many people must share a phobia before it becomes a social institution. It depends on the context. Similarly, a phobia or obsessional worry can have elements of rationality. It is perfectly rational to worry about getting sick, but health anxiety OCD (what used to be called "hypochondria") is a neurosis in which the emotion of worry outstrips rational fear. Finally, a taboo can be encoded in a law (e.g., a ban on public nudity), placing it within a rational-legal framework. What separates an obsessional worry from rational fear, taboo from law is

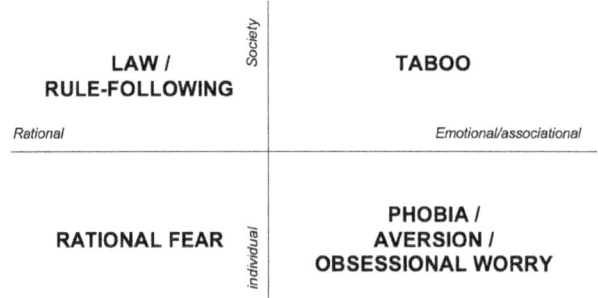

Figure 2 A classification scheme of avoidance behaviors on the axes of individual-society and rational-emotional. Figure by author.

when people obey the prohibition *primarily* for emotional reasons, not working from first principles. They are felt, not reasoned.

The Purpose of Taboos

Much of the anthropological literature has attempted to understand not only what taboos are, but also why they exist. Most anthropologists have adopted symbolic approaches: Frazer, Smith, Douglas, Van Gennep, Lévi-Strauss, and more recently Valeri (2000). Their perspectives have varied, but they have all seen taboos as protective of categories of meaning within a social structure. Offering a variation on this theme are those, like Simoons (1961) and DeBoer (1987), who take an identity-based approach and focus attention on how taboos separate groups from one another, thereby playing an instrumental role in the development and reproduction of ethnic, gender, and other social categories. Such explanations are in sync with Allan and Burridge's (2006, p. 1) argument that taboos by and large reflect bodily anxieties, and thus sense of self (an issue important to Valeri (2000) as well), or Fessler and Navarrete's (2003) contention that it's all about "normative moralization." On the other hand, functionalists like Harris (1974) have tended to see taboos as adaptive, usually by preventing disease or enhancing ecological fitness.

There is no "correct" way of understanding a taboo. All these frameworks are helpful in understanding different aspects of taboos across contexts. However, I offer another perspective, one that draws upon Radcliffe-Brown (1939) and Godelier's (2011) reformulation of Lévi-Strauss (1969): Taboos protect not only the body and the self, as Valeri (2000) and Allan and Burridge (2006) argue, but also *proper social reproduction*. Social reproduction encompasses not just biological reproduction (sex, pregnancy, birth, and raising a child), but also the material reproduction of life – gathering food, building houses, cooking, fashioning clothing, eating – and the passing down of knowledge and traditions. All of these activities require human conscious interaction with the material world. Social reproduction is the process in which the past, present, and future of a society fit together. It is how values and identities are made and unmade. As such, social reproduction is a potentially dangerous moment as much as it is a necessary one. To be done properly, certain restrictions must apply.

While taboos come in all sorts, most relate to four types of activities: eating, sex, speaking, and social/biological transformation (birth, puberty/adulthood, marriage, pregnancy, death). Each plays a vital role in social reproduction – biologically, materially, or socially. Because these activities are so important, they attract significant emotional energy, the raw material from which to construct taboos. Through associations with existing social structures, taboos guide processes of social reproduction by negation. They build fences around these four key types of activities.

My perspective is not entirely novel. Kahn (1986), wrote about taboos on taro cultivation by pregnant/breastfeeding women among the Wamira in New Guinea: "The cultivation of taro by men and the birth and nurture of children by women are occasions for men and women to demonstrate their creative powers ... Taboos are created and maintained to regulate and minimize conflict between female and male domains of creation." (Kahn, 1986, p. 118)

Kahn's "reproduction" hypothesis, like mine, focuses on the process of creation and the proper functioning of social life. It is similar to the structural functionalism of Radcliffe-Brown (1939), who maintained that taboos protect and support social structures. But the perspective I adopt draws attention to what was arguably structural functionalism's greatest blind spot: the lack of conflict, contradiction, and domination. As Kahn implies, while taboos regulate social tensions, they also facilitate domination. This is why I write that taboos protect *proper* social reproduction. What is proper? Proper to whom? Who gets to decide? And – what is particularly important for archaeologists to consider – what happens during cultural change, when taboos may come into conflict with new social structures, human impulses, economic/environmental conditions, technologies, or external influences? These questions force us to consider how power and domination enter into the equation.

In fact, taboos are very much a part of power structures. Taboos can mark and maintain distinctions between social categories with differential access to power. Christine Hastorf (2016, pp. 181–187) specifically draws attention to gender taboos. While one may see food taboos on women as protective of socially meaningful gender categories or even health during pregnancy (Speth, 2009, pp. 109–112; Henrich and Henrich, 2010), Hastorf (2016) argues that oftentimes such taboos restrict women from important nutrients and calories, especially animal fat and protein (see also Zvelebil, 2000):

> The female food taboos had more than a nutritive impact; they reinforced the political positions of certain individuals, constantly re[i]nstating their place within the political hierarchy. These taboos regulated the female body as well as women's place in society. The prohibitions, while ostensibly spiritual in origin and certainly naturalized within community ontologies, perpetuated and naturalized gender inequalities and political hierarchies, reflected especially in the hearths and ovens that separately cooked male and female food within every household. (Hastorf, 2016, p. 185)

Similarly, sumptuary rules and the taboos that surround them may limit certain foods to people of higher classes (Hastorf, 2016, p. 182). Alternatively, powerful people may be subject to additional taboos, such as the avoidance of otherwise good-to-eat eels among the *sikerie* ("shamans") among the Mentawi people in Indonesia (Singh and Henrich, 2020) or the king of the Mamprusi in Ghana avoiding goat and other animals associated with earth-shrines (Dietler, 2001, p. 87). Taboos may also be lifted for powerful people; brother-sister sex, for example, among elites in ancient Hawaii or Egypt. In their concern for proper social reproduction, taboos participate in a broader process of domination and resistance in a variety of ways, but often through marking through distinction.

Taboos and their transgressions are therefore political. Consider, for example, gender norms in 21st-century America and the taboos that ensconce them. Abiding by these taboos or encoding them in law (e.g., enforcing bathroom access based on chromosomal sex) advances a political agenda concerning sexuality, the family, and personhood. Transgression can also be political. Especially when they have the force of law behind them, violating taboos – entering the "wrong" gendered bathroom or sitting at the "Whites Only" lunch counter at a Greensboro Woolworth's – can sometimes lead to broader sociopolitical transformation.

A Definition

To close this section, I want to revisit my definition of taboo from an earlier work: "In a general sense, a taboo is a form of culturally prescribed avoidance of a thing or an activity that is surrounded by a high degree of social energy. This avoidance is bound by a moralized cosmological order – an idea of what is right and wrong based on fundamental principles that appear to people as immutable." (Price, 2021, p. 92)

I stick to that definition here, but offer a few additional points. First, a taboo is a special type of ritual. While some aspects of taboo avoidance can be argued to be rational, what makes a taboo a meaningful social category is its reliance on associative magical thinking. Second, taboos are social institutions, ones that evolve as a result of the dialectic between thought and action, ideology and practice. Third, one can understand the meaning or purpose of taboos in general in many ways. They protect and divide the self from the non-self. They form barriers around dangerous liminalities and uncategorizable things. But they are also concerned with proper social reproduction and the politics that surrounds it.

4 Meat Is Good to Taboo

Having laid out an anthropological approach to taboos and provided a working definition, the rest of this Element will focus specifically on food taboos. However, before delving into the methodological issues and case studies related to the archaeological analysis of food taboo, we must approach the question raised in Section 1, a question that hangs like a veil over so much anthropological and archaeological work on taboos: Why do most food taboos involve meat?

Before going further, I want to make it clear that I am not saying that *all* food taboos apply to meat. For one thing, taboos can apply to food prepared or acquired in the wrong way or by the wrong person, rather than to the actual substance of the food itself. For example, food cooked by menstruating women can be taboo to men in some cultures (e.g., Meigs, 1984, p. 21). Some taboos apply to plants. A good example is a taboo on gathering a certain type of red (and thus blood-like) berries by menstruating women of the Hadza in Tanzania. First reported by James Woodburn (1964), the taboo was still being followed several decades later (Power, 2015; Fitzpatrick, 2018). Similarly, taboos on feminine-referencing foods exist for Hua men of highland New Guinea (Meigs, 1984). Other plant-related taboos focus on the mind-altering affects of certain compounds. One example is the proscription of alcohol (*khamr*) in Islam (Quran 5:90). Perhaps another example is the use of restricted or illicit drugs in American culture. As is the case for alcohol in Islam, calling drugs "taboo" is complicated by the legal structures that surround them, their toxicity, and their potential for addiction. These are rational reasons for avoidance. But people avoid heroin or even tobacco for reasons that pertain to social identity (being a "user" or "addict" or part of the "wrong crowd") and emotions (disgust at the smell of smoke, fear of loss of sense of self). Seen in this light, drug avoidance can appear as a taboo.

These examples notwithstanding, as Fessler and Navarette (2003) aver, "meat is good to taboo." Why? A functionalist might argue that meat spoils easily and can cause disease (see discussion in Fessler and Navarrete, 2003). True, spoiled meat can cause a host of complications: listeriosis, *Escherichia coli* and *Salmonella* poisoning, trichinosis, brucellosis, campylobacterioris, tapeworms, roundworms, pinworms, botulism, and more. Yet it should be clear by now that such explanations are simplistic and partial. Fessler and Navarette (2003, pp. 19–20) dig a bit deeper, suggesting that the tendency to place taboos around meat reflects an evolved sense of hesitancy around meat. In contrast to poisonous plants and fungi that have evolved defenses, spoiled meat does not always advertise itself clearly. They cite studies demonstrating that stimulation of or damage to the amygdala, which helps regulate emotions and memory, can alter meat consumption behaviors in macaques and domestic cats. This suggests attraction/aversion to meat is deeply seated in mammalian emotions. While it may be subject to powerful feelings, positive and negative, humans and many other animals, as a general rule, crave meat and tend to prefer it to safer foods.

Such ambiguity between disgust and craving may well be the ultimate evolutionary reason for a love–fear relationship. But if culture is to have any explanatory power, this thesis remains only a partial explanation. It is also critical to consider the special place meat holds in the human experience. Meat is not just craved; in many cultures, eating without meat is not even a proper meal. Meat tends to be the centerpiece of feasts, ritually charged meals that can reproduce or challenge sociopolitical power. Feasts often require a riot of meat, far more than can be eaten even after guests gorge themselves silly (Twiss, 2008, p. 423). In many cultures, the acquisition of meat through big-game hunting is ritualized in reference to its capacity to reproduce masculinity through productive violence; frequently, it also reproduces the domination of women by men (Fiddes, 1991, p. 146; Russell, 2012, pp. 155–160). In other words, the killing and eating animals is part of the proper reproduction of society.

In short, meat comes to the table dripping from head to toe in symbolism. Even Harris, the champion of functionalist explanations, acknowledges the symbolic value of meat: "[A]ll over the world ... people honor and crave animal foods more than plant foods and are willing to lavish a disproportionate share of their energy and wealth on producing them" (Harris, 1985a, p. 22). Harris is on point, but he proceeds to argue that the reason meat is so symbolically powerful is because it is nutritionally valuable. This explanation, like a meatless meal, may leave one full, but never satisfied. It relegates all the sentiments surrounding meat to *Zweckrationalität*.

Meat's grip on the human imagination lies in the symbolic value attached to animals themselves. I am in agreement with Russell (2012, p. 156), Fiddes (1991), and Valeri (2000, pp. 175–176) that this value lies ultimately in the conflicting feelings over killing animals – guilt, power, ontological superiority, moral uncertainty:

> The symbolic significance of meat probably derives from the highly charged act of killing animate beings not so different from us. Nick Fiddes (1991) sees killing and eating animals as a way of demonstrating human superiority over nature, whereas Brian Morris (1998, p. 186) argues that for subsistence hunters killing animals is not about exercising power *over* nature, but incorporating the powers *of* nature, the life force of the animals (Russell, 2012, p. 156).

Humans recognize an ontological proximity to animals. Killing them feels like a betrayal, murder, or even cannibalism. We kill animals to satisfy our biologically driven craving for their meat, to harvest the symbolic power that killing and eating them confers, and to reproduce proper social relations through actions that are dangerously violent and tinged with bloodlust. This craving, and the dangers that surround it, confronts an inner guilt that we, whether butcher, hunter, slaughterer, or supermarket shopper, feel deep down. People have developed a number of tactics to combat this guilt. Valeri observed that Huaulu owners of animal traps never participated in the butchering of their prey and that laughing was strictly forbidden during the process of dismemberment and butchery (Valeri, 2000, pp. 172–173). Our own society, and many others, finds recourse in a hierarchy of beings. Though many animal rights proponents argue eloquently against it, most of us (try to) tell ourselves that animals are less than human and thus killable. Virtually all societies or segments of societies follow rituals that regulate how to kill animals (e.g., kosher or halal slaughter). And they enact taboos to restrict certain types of consumption and killing.

The power of animals and the reasons they are so good to taboo may reflect, on the deepest level, an evolutionary hesitancy around a beneficial-but-potentially dangerous food. But the more proximate reason is cultural, deriving from the collective emotional tension stemming from desire, guilt, and ontological and existential anxiety. Meat is a substance able to reproduce social relations and identities and satisfy hunger; but, because its acquisition is violent, even murderous, it also has the danger of stripping us of our humanity. That tension becomes ramified into symbolic value, and from there into cultural structures like taboos.

Cannibalism

The reader will note that I have largely avoided discussion of what is the most pervasive food taboo across the globe: the consumption of human flesh. I have done so for three reasons. First, especially in ethnographic and historical cases, accusations of cannibalism can be difficult to verify. Because it is such a powerful taboo cross-culturally, cannibalism constitutes a common pejorative thrown at unknown or enemy groups. The "barbarians living just beyond the horizon" are cannibals. Second, cases of cannibalism are so sensationalized – again, in large part because they violate such a powerful taboo – that to give them significant attention in this Element would suck the air out of the rest of the examples. I did not want this to become a cannibalism Element. Third, archaeological, historical, and ethnographic cases of cannibalism are covered extensively elsewhere and are subject to significant debate (Sanday, 1986; Villa, 1992; Rhodes, 1997; Rautman and Fenton, 2005; Saladié and Rodríguez-Hidalgo, 2017; Winchcombe, 2023).

That said, I should say a few words on cannibalism, which will ultimately help us understand why meat is so good to taboo. First, the taboo on cannibalism is universal in that, even in cases in which human flesh is eaten, the act of doing so is surrounded by heightened affect and, more often than not, rituals to separate it from everyday consumption It is an *abnormal* act. Endo- or exocannibalism, for example, are often components of mortuary or other highly charged rituals – consuming the flesh of deceased loved ones to recycle their bodies into the next generation and free their spirits (Whitfield *et al.*, 2008); eating the bodies of enemies to humiliate and terrorize them, or to embody the animalized (and thus socially liminal) condition of the warrior. In other situations, people resort to the meat of humans only in desperation. And then there are the highly deviant individuals (e.g., Jeffrey Dahmer) who, by eating the flesh of other people, turn themselves into criminals or pariahs.

Second, we can think of cannibalism as a keystone taboo, similar to the incest taboo in Lévi-Strauss (1969). This idea is quite old. Durkheim (1995), for example, saw cannibalism as the avoidance of eating something like oneself, and thereby drew the connection between incest and cannibalism clearly. He reasoned that many, if not most, food taboos boil down to it. Others have argued in a similar vein (e.g., Valeri, 2000). That cannibalism is a universal and keystone taboo, likely as old or older than *Homo sapiens* as a species, can help us make sense of the prevalence of taboos on meat. Indeed, emic and etic explanations of food taboos often reference cannibalism ("we cannot eat dogs because to do so is tantamount to cannibalism"). To eat animals is dangerous because animals are like us, and to eat each other is unimaginable.

5 Food Taboos in Archaeology

A Job for Archaeologists

If we consider the main domains of human activity to which taboos apply cross-culturally – sexuality (including modesty in dress), speaking, death, and eating – food taboos are arguably the most visible in the archaeological record. Archaeological indications of food practices are manifold. Much of what we excavate, from ceramic sherds to animal bones to charred seeds, reflects eating and cooking. Many other types of artifacts (e.g., lithics) and depositional features (hearths) are connected to food production. Unsurprisingly, then, there is a copious body of literature detailing foodways in the archaeological record reflecting research conducted by experts in various sub-fields and specialized techniques: zooarchaeology, archaeobotany, ceramic analysis, residue analysis, stable isotope analysis, among others (e.g., Bray, 2003; Fu and Altmann, 2014; Hastorf, 2016; Peres, 2017; Twiss, 2019; Jaffe, 2023).

As a zooarchaeologist, what I'm about to write might sound conceited: Zooarchaeology is uniquely and ideally situated to contribute to an archaeology of taboos. This is for two reasons. First, animal bones are recovered in large numbers from archaeological sites, even from contexts with poor preservation or those that are hastily excavated. Simply put, we can say a lot about what types of meat people ate. Second, cross-culturally, most food taboos apply to meat. This does not mean that zooarchaeology should have exclusive access to the taboos of the past; archaeology is always better when multiple sub-disciplines combine forces. But it does mean that most archaeological discussions of food taboos derive from faunal analysis and that zooarchaeology, especially "traditional zooarchaeology," is often an ideal starting place to begin an archaeology of taboos.

That said, several analytical challenges present themselves to an archaeology of taboos. They range from the typical issues pertaining to distribution, deposition, preservation, and taphonomy, to a more epistemological conundrum – how do we collect evidence of absence?

The Archaeological Detection of Food Taboos

Bones do not come out of the ground screaming they are taboo. That is an unfortunate fact for archaeologists. In very few cases, and in no prehistoric case, can one identify a food taboo unambiguously. The archaeology of food taboos is necessarily one that relies on the spice of conjecture. For those working in prehistory, an archaeology of taboos will undoubtedly be unsatisfying to hard-nosed empiricists allergic to speculation. There is not much that can be done to appease them other than by giving voice to their credible concerns. Still, I argue, along with Fowles (2008), that pursuing an archaeology of taboos is important, however shaky the empirical ground. If we foreclose on informed speculation, we write out important features of past human cultures.

Historical archaeology is much better situated for the study of food taboos. In these cases, we can use the weight of written or oral records to guide hypotheses and expectations. That does not mean that archaeology can only serve to test the historical record. Rather, archaeology informs us, through the material record, how and under what circumstances taboos evolved, were practiced, were violated, and ultimately disappeared.

Even under the best circumstances, food taboos can be difficult to detect due to discard patterns. If food taboos extend merely to eating a food, and not to killing an animal, zooarchaeologists will be hard-pressed to identify it. Reichel-Dolmatoff (1978, p. 289) noted that Desana groups in Brazil observed a taboo on tapir meat. Yet they nevertheless killed and smoked tapirs to trade with other groups. Unless the Desana traders were meticulous in removing the entire tapir carcasses, the archaeological record would contain evidence of killing and cooking these taboo animals. Similarly, parts of taboo animals could be used as ritual paraphernalia or for making non-food items (e.g., bone used for making tools).

In addition to complicated discard patterns, rules over who must follow taboos and when are often quite variable. A person may have to abide by a taboo in one situation, but not another. Food taboos often apply to women (and sometimes their husbands) who are pregnant, post-partum, menstruating, and breastfeeding (Henrich and Henrich, 2010; Fitzpatrick, 2018). Ritual participants are another group of people to which food taboos frequently apply. The *kambanji* novices in Turner's (1967, p. 234) analysis of initiation rites among the Ndembu of Zambia could not eat a host of animals including zebra, striped mice, bushbuck, kingfisher, and other animals with striped or spotted appearance, the consumption of which was believed to cause leprosy. In Meigs' (1984) illuminating ethnography of food and sex taboos among the Hua in highland New Guinea, what was off-limits was dictated by a concept of a fluid-like life-force substance called *nu* that is abundant in fertile women and depleted in young men. To protect and increase their *nu*, young male initiates observe a host of taboos, especially to foods that resemble, smell like, or otherwise reference female reproduction.

All of these are temporary states, difficult to distinguish archaeologically. Similarly, taboos might only apply, or be lifted, during certain rituals. The Lenten fast, the forty-day taboo on meat observed by Catholics after Good Friday, is an example.

More permanent taboos also pose difficulties. From an archaeological perspective, taboos (general taboos) affecting the whole group are the easiest to observe. The pig taboo in in Judaism and Islam is a prime example. But, cross-culturally, food taboos can apply to many different types of people. It is common for powerful people to have specific taboos. Shamans, monks, and other holy people, for example, often abide by "costly" taboos on meat and sex (see e.g., Singh and Henrich, 2020). In the northern part of Kiriwina (Trobriand Islands), boiled/stewed foods are taboo to chiefs, but they are the only ones for whom stingray and flatfish are not forbidden (Meyer-Rochow, 2009). All types of meat are taboo to members of the Brahmin caste in India, at least in theory, but not to other castes (Caplan, 2008; Khara, Riedy, and Ruby, 2020). In other cases, different foods may be acceptable to different age groups or gender categories. It is only for the old men among the Gidra of New Guinea that pig fetuses are not taboo (Akimichi, 1998). While it may be possible to conduct a contextual analysis of food remains – for example, food remains from a shrine or an elite domestic structure associated – the messy reality of the archaeological rarely affords such opportunities to explore foodways across the full range of social variation.

The reason it would be difficult to detect these taboos in the archaeological record is because the people following them would be unlikely to present significantly different discard patterns from those who do not. We must remember that most archaeological data, and especially most archaeobotanical and zooarchaeological data, derive from secondary deposits that are time- and space-averaged palimpsests (Lyman, 2003). Furthermore, they are usually waste deposits in areas of a settlement specifically chosen to receive discarded items and garbage. This may not perfectly reflect diet; food taboos usually apply to killing, eating, or touching the meat of an animal, not to garbage into which all manner of unholy things may be deposited. Moreover, if multiple groups (gender, ethnicity, etc.) use a space for disposal, any taboo dependent on one of these identities will be difficult to detect.

The strength or power of a taboo is conditional, meaning that some taboos are more likely to be "imprinted" in the archaeological record than others. In much of Polynesia, the power of a certain type of taboo more-or-less directly corresponded to the *mana* of the person who issued it – and indeed, the power to declare taboo was the very definition of chiefly power (Steiner, 1956, p. 39). Weak chiefs issued weak taboos that were often violated. Other factors can strengthen or diminish the power of taboos. Taboos evolve, changing in meaning and strength over time (Price, 2021). Politics may come into play. In Hawaii, food taboos constituted a battleground between the priests and the king, part of a larger struggle for political power. In 1819, Kamehameha II defied the priesthood by dining with women, an act that was *kapu*. In the process, the king effectively lifted the food taboos (Webb, 1965). An archaeological study of Hawaiian feasts before and after this decree would be an interesting one to pursue from the perspective of gendered taboos.

Transgression is a regular feature of taboos and, indeed, may be quite common. Despite its clear injunction in the Torah and Quran, many 21st century Jews and Muslims eat pork. Reform Judaism, which dates back to 19th century Germany and is the most popular form of Judaism in the United States, explicitly rejects the Leviticus food taboos. Similarly, many Muslims drink alcohol and many Brahmins eat meat, often in contexts concealed from their family or community (Khara, Riedy, and Ruby, 2020). In fact, any community is likely to be a mix abiders and transgressors. Paradoxically, violation of a taboo, whether in reality, myth, or fiction, can strengthen a taboo by inspiring disgust, horror, and vilification of the perpetrators. What would the taboo on cannibalism be without Jeffrey Dahmer, the Donner Party, zombie films, or Hannibal Lecter? Yet as complicated as this makes identifying taboo, it is also a place where archaeology has something important to contribute. Violating taboos is often not spoken of. It is actively suppressed in everyday conversation and historical records. The material record is often the only proof that it occurred.

Fowles (2008) rightly points out that taboos are defined by absences, and archaeological reasoning tends to cut against treating absence of evidence as evidence of absence (see also Russell, 2018, p. 15). After all, bones may not enter the archaeological record for all sorts of reasons: for example, extirpation of a species, the cessation of hunting for cultural or economic reasons, the appearance of a more reliable and abundant food source. Even if a species is consumed, species-dependent processing or discard patterns, such as particular cooking practices or the need to remove larger bones from near houses (Meadow, 1980), might make that species practically invisible to archaeologists.

Ethnoarchaeology of Taboo

Ethnoarchaeological studies of food taboos are badly needed. It is only by studying the material record taboos under known conditions that we can hope to understand, or at least come to grips with, the various complexities I have covered. Unfortunately, there has been little work in this vein, with one major exception: Politis and Saunders' (2002) ethnoarchaeological study among Nukak communities in the Amazon (see also Politis, 2016).

Politis and Saunders (2002) provide a template for doing an archaeology of taboos that should serve as both a beacon of inspiration and a shadow of caution for archaeologists without the benefit of rich ethnographic information to fill in the gaps. On the one hand, they provide an example of the ways in which zooarchaeological data, specifically species counts and distribution of elements, can inform an understanding of taboos, even for sub-groups within a population. For instance, the white-lipped peccary is taboo to Nukak women and children, but not men. Many women displayed "great discomfort at the idea of eating peccary or smelling its smoked meat" (2002, p. 119). When men hunt and eat the animal, they are careful to keep the meat away from household spaces, typically cooking and consuming peccaries at a distance from their residential camp. The result is a pattern of butchery and discard spatially distinct from that of other animals, whose bones would be found close to residential units.

A more specific description of typical peccary hunting and consumption patterns reveals how zooarchaeological information can reflect nuances in food taboos across space (Figure 3). Following a successful hunt, men typically remove peccary heads and leave them at a temporary butchery location near the kill site. This pattern of field butchery, in which low-utility parts are left near kill sites is common among hunters, especially of larger animals. Zooarchaeologists have understood this since Theodore White (1952) first postulated it as an explanation for unexpected bone frequencies at archaeological sites (for a review of the history of the concept, see Lyman, 1985).

Following primary butchery, Nukak hunters bring the peccary carcass to a grilling spot just outside the residential camp, where it is cooked, processed

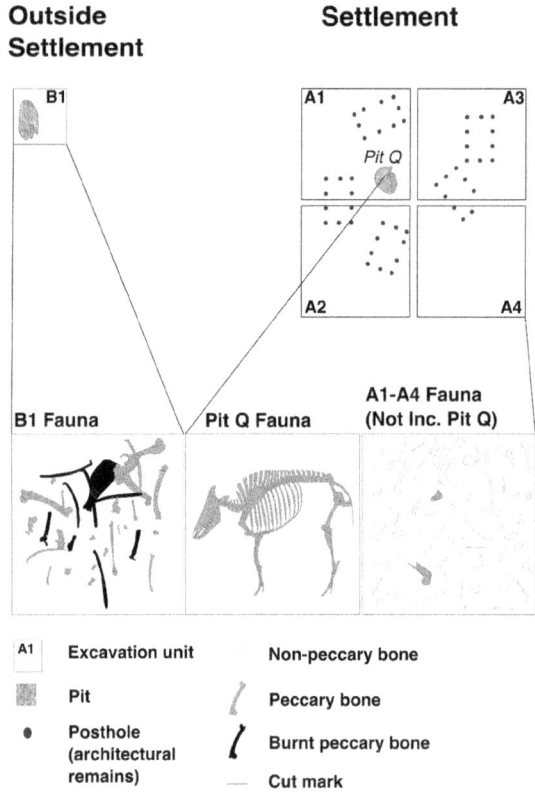

Figure 3 Hypothetical archaeological excavation of a Nukak settlement. Squares show excavation trenches A1-A4 and B1 and the faunal remains recovered. The pattern of finds represents the material signature of a taboo on white-lipped peccary, applicable only to women and children. See text for details. Figure by author.

for marrow, and eaten. Most long bones, ribs, and vertebra are deposited around these grilling spots, and that is where Politis and Saunders recovered them archaeologically (2002, pp. 118–119). Because they are in close proximity to the residential camp, and because they are likely used repeatedly, these sites stand a higher chance of being detected and excavated, even though their archaeological impact is lower than residential areas. Still, the location of the grilling spots at a remove from residential sites means that archaeologists would only recover them if they excavated trenches in lower-density areas at the edges, or just off the edges, of the site.

The Nukak woman/child taboo on white-lipped peccary, therefore, should result in a relatively interpretable pattern: Peccary remains (minus crania) should be found near the edges of habitation sites, where there would be evidence for cooking but not architecture. However, the picture is not as neat as one might like. An archaeologist might find peccary remains *inside* a residential camp. Small bones like phalanges or long bone fragments may find their way into the residential camp area due to dog or other post-depositional transport processes. Complicating things further, people sometimes keep immature peccaries as pets. Though they are not eaten, when they die, their remains usually enter the archaeological record within the residential camps. Thus, one would have to modify the expectations for an archaeological signature of this taboo: White-lipped peccary remains in significant proportions should be found *with evidence of cooking and butchery* at the edges of habitation sites, but very low proportions of *small/highly fragmented* peccary bones (say, less than 2% by Number of Identified Specimens (NISP)) may be found in proximity to residential units. *Articulate skeletons of peccaries lacking cooking or butchery marks* are also expected near residential units.

It would be relatively straightforward to apply this pattern *deductively*. That is, if one approached the archaeological record with this template of zooarchaeological and spatial data in mind, there would be a good chance of establishing a gendered taboo on peccary meat in the past. Furthermore, if, say, one wished to track the evolution of Nukak peccary taboos, one could excavate habitation sites from the past few centuries to discern changing patterns. However, it would be quite difficult to identify the taboo *inductively*. That is, a zooarchaeologist without any prior knowledge of Nukak foodways would be unlikely to conclude from the zooarchaeological data that a taboo on peccary meat applied exclusively to women and children. It would not, however, be impossible. A bit of ethnographic analogy and some informed speculation could lead a creative-minded zooarchaeologist to draw the correct inference. However, they would be hard-pressed to convince a skeptic.

Nevertheless, the spatial distribution of faunal remains does reveal, if not taboos, per se, then *unexpected* patterns. In a later article, Politis (2016) compared the ethnoarchaeological faunal patterns of the Nukak to a nearby group, the Hotï. The latter followed fewer food taboos, but disposed of food waste in a structured fashion, often separating the remains into piles specific to animal type. Politis attended to how these taboos and other cultural ideals could be read from these atypical discard patterns, or "bonescapes." Indeed, archaeologists often encounter unexpected bonescapes: for example, the lack of wild boar bones at Çatalhöyük (Russell, 2018). Archaeologists can also bring unexpected zooarchaeological patterns into conversation with other lines of evidence, such as art. For example, Bonomo *et al.* (2021) found an unexpected pattern in their contrast of faunal remains and ceramic depictions of animals at sites belonging to the Goya-Malabrigo tradition in northeastern Argentina. Generally speaking, animals depicted were not consumed. Similarly, Peters and Schmidt (2004) noted contrasts between the faunal remains and stone carvings of animals at the iconic site of Göbekli Tepe in southeast Turkey. While we may not be able to diagnose taboos from these patterns with certainty, they do implicate powerful ideological structures ensconcing human-animal relations – situations in which taboos often develop and persist.

Politis and Saunders' ethnography is informative in many other ways. Nukak taboos on piranha, deer, and jaguar offer additional complexities, but also tantalizing options for zooarchaeologists to interpret their data. In these cases, the meat of the animal is taboo, but the carcasses are not. In fact, Nukak catch piranha not to eat, but in order to use their teeth to fashion knives, carving tools, and hair-cutting implements. Piranha remains therefore enter into the zooarchaeological record – just not as food. Similarly, while deer and jaguar are not hunted, the Nukak make flutes from deer tibia and jaguar humeri that they scavenge. It is taboo to kill or eat these animals; it is not taboo to touch their bones (Politis and Saunders, 2002, p. 124). This pattern bears similarity to other cultural contexts. For example, horses in medieval Europe were taboo to eat, but their bones were used in tool manufacture and dead horses were skinned for hides (Serjeantson, 2000, p. 184). Taboos may apply to touching an animal, killing it, eating its flesh, or touching products derived from its body parts. Sometimes taboos apply to all of these aspects; sometimes to only one or two. While difficult to discern, these rules impact a taboo's archaeological signature.

Again, a deductive approach – that is, analyzing the assemblage with the prior knowledge of the taboo and the expected pattern – is more compelling than an inductive one, in which the zooarchaeologist has no prior knowledge of specific expectations. "Discovering" inductively the piranha, deer, or jaguar taboos at a Nukak archaeological site would require careful analysis of body part representation and cut marks, the latter in order to differentiate marks made by skinning/tool manufacture and butchery. This is possible, but would require large sample sizes (on the order of at least 1,000 specimens identified to these taxa), extensive documentation of taphonomic factors affecting the assemblage, and excavation and sieving protocols to ensure high rates of recovery. In addition, identifying these taboos would require, as emphasized already, a fair amount of speculation informed by ethnographic analogy and some creativity. In other words, the zooarchaeologist would have to exercise the creative (associational) and analytical (rational) aspects of their cognition.

Moving Forward with an Archaeology of Food Taboos

Where does this leave us? We know that food taboos are an essential part of the human condition and we can observe the diversity of food taboos ethnographically. An archaeology of food taboos is therefore, I would argue, a critical component of any approach to past foodways. In particular, because meat is most often subject to taboo, and because animal bones are among the most common finds at archaeological sites, zooarchaeology is uniquely positioned to contribute to the conversation. Yet there are major methodological hurdles.

There are some who would take the position, arguably more analytically sound, that food taboos are perched upon the higher rungs of Hawkes' (1954) "ladder of inference." Archaeologists, they would argue, must come to grips with the fact that most food taboos will remain invisible to them. Just as we cannot reconstruct the languages of Upper Paleolithic Eurasia or discern what, if any, clothing *Homo erectus* wore, the "forest of taboos" (Valeri, 2000) which many of our archaeological subjects inhabited will remain uncharted. At best we can hope that future methodological techniques will enable us to detect them in new ways. Fowles, for example, despite pushing for an archaeology of taboos, adopts an equanimous pessimism, bordering on the blasé: "We will never know whether it was taboo for a Cro-Magnon hunter to eat the game he himself killed or whether certain behaviors were forbidden to a Natufian woman during menstruation ... Fair enough." (Fowles, 2008, p. 33).

Fair enough, indeed. But there is no need to bow to defeatism or to the *deus ex machina* of future technology. We need a way forward. Fowles suggests the search for "conspicuous absence" in the archaeological record, even while recognizing that such a prescription may be as much a cop-out as an insight (Fowles, 2008, p. 33). He recommends archaeologists develop "criteria of conspicuousness" – for example, the rapid disappearance of a food (or other tabooed thing) over time or abrupt spatial differences (Fowles, 2008, p. 33). But when is an absence conspicuous or unexpected? What is "rapid" or "abrupt?" One simply sets up a fight on the battlefield of adjectives.

On the other hand, Fowles' approach may be the only possibility in prehistoric contexts and other cases in which archaeologists approach taboos *inductively*. His approach has its benefits. It forces our gaze onto the singular importance of context. The archaeology of taboos is not so much about finds, or lack thereof, as it is a careful *reading* of material culture patterns (à la Hodder, 1986) within their spatio-temporal frameworks. This requires engagement with, and a tolerance for, informed speculation. Admittedly, we may not know if a *specific* taboo existed in the past, but we do know that *some* taboos did, since they exist in all known human cultures. We can therefore speculate as to which taboos existed and how they operated.

A deductive approach to taboos stands on sturdier ground. The use of direct historical analogs and other *a priori* information allows archaeologists to lay out specific expectations for patterning in the faunal and other material cultural records. There are some risks. The many studies of the origins of the pig taboo in the southern Levant in the Iron Age have made much use of the direct historical approach, but can be accused of anachronistic projection. We cannot assume that an absence in the past means the same thing as an absence today. Nevertheless, it is within historical archaeology that we have the best chance of doing the most analytically sound work on food taboos. Moreover, such analyses can help us better refine our interpretive and analytical frameworks, for under a deductive approach, we can ask specific questions about transgression and context. In the next section, I draw on several case studies to show how this is possible.

6 Case Studies

Having covered what food taboos are, as an anthropological phenomenon, and the methodological issues pertaining to the archaeological study of them, we are now in a position to examine a few case studies (Figure 4). The reader will note that all of the taboos covered here involve meat – as noted in the previous section, not only is meat good to taboo, but it is also good for archaeological study as bones are among the most common finds in the course of excavation.

We can divide the archaeology of taboo roughly into historic and prehistoric approaches, the latter conducted without the benefit of written or oral documentation. Historical approaches have many advantages because we can study

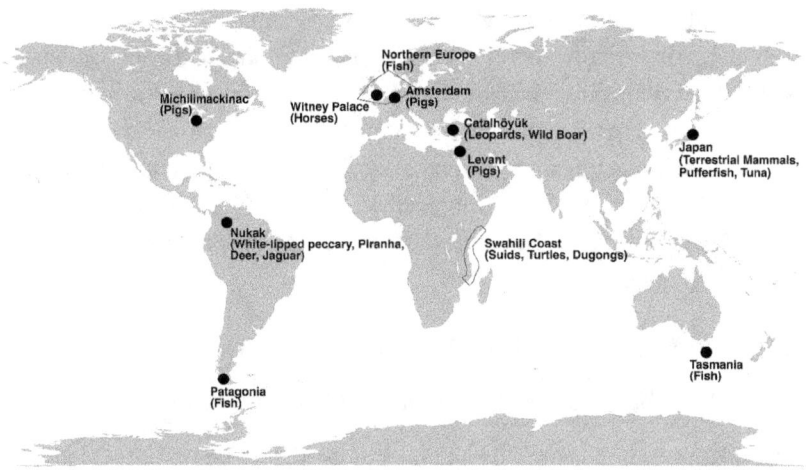

Figure 4 Case studies, including the animals under taboo. Figure by author.

taboos *deductively*. Archaeologists of taboo find themselves in more troubled waters when working in prehistoric contexts, especially those dating so far back in time as to strain the credulity of cultural connections to the present. On the one hand, we can be sure that people as far back as the Upper Paleolithic (and probably much earlier) followed taboos. On the other hand, we must take up the awkward task of searching for "conspicuous absences," as Fowles (2008) put it, without a guide for where to start. We must work *inductively*.

We return to the question: what makes an absence "conspicuous" enough to warrant our suspicion of a taboo? Archaeologists working in prehistoric contexts often fall back on functionalist interpretations informed by human behavioral ecology. Food sources can be ranked according to their returns (in calories, fat, protein, etc.) and the effort required to obtain them. Ostensible cases of food taboos in prehistoric contexts generally start from observing the absence of a particular species that, because of its rank and availability, would be expected in the faunal assemblage. The diligent zooarchaeologist then examines environmental, ecological, taphonomic, or economic explanations for the absence. Finding none, the zooarchaeologist is then free to play the taboo card by the oft-employed, if frequently criticized, archaeological trope "if it ain't practical, it's ritual." Before casting stones, I would note that tropes are not necessarily incorrect and that rituals/taboos are a part of the human experience that often defies simple calculations of caloric efficiency. While it may be simplistic, the material signatures of rituals are, indeed, often conspicuous because they do not make sense from a functionalist perspective.

It is worth pointing out a slight irony, however. Approaching taboos in this functionalist framework works from the opposite direction as functionalist anthropological interpretations of taboo, which posit that taboos are ultimately adaptive (e.g., Harris, 1974; Ross, 1978; Henrich and Henrich, 2010). Archaeological functionalists assume a food taboo is discoverable because it is non-practical (e.g., in terms of immediate caloric efficiency), but anthropological functionalists explain the existence of the taboo as practical (e.g., ecologically efficient).

Finding Taboos Without Writing: Prehistoric Archaeology

Hunting and Taboos at Neolithic Çatalhöyük

Nerissa Russell, in her pathbreaking *Social Zooarchaeology* (2012), encouraged zooarchaeologists to loosen the straps on the straightjacket of a strictly empirical approach, without abandoning it altogether, in order to pursue topics such as food taboos. Unsurprisingly, Russell has been a leading voice in the zooarchaeology of taboos in the deep past (see esp. Russell, 2012, pp. 29–44), primarily through her work at the Neolithic site of Çatalhöyük in central Turkey.

Russell (2018) attempts to connect unexpected relative frequencies in the Çatalhöyük (ca. 7100–6000 BC) faunal assemblage to Neolithic art and ostensible ritual paraphernalia. She draws on a diverse array of species indigenous to the region and occasionally also includes notes on cut marks and the treatment of bones. Leopards are a prime example. Leopards were depicted in artwork at Çatalhöyük and contemporaneous sites. Some paintings show people dressed in leopard skins. But leopard remains are conspicuously absent. The only identified leopard bone – out of roughly one million identified fragments – is a pierced 3rd phalanx (or claw). Excavators recovered this unique faunal find in a burial containing the site's only plastered skull (Russell, 2018, pp. 16–17). Russell argues that the complete absence of leopard remains from quotidian deposits, and the exceptional rarity of leopard remains in general, could be an indication that there was a taboo on killing jaguars. This begs a number of questions: What was the identity of the individual buried – was the person a ritual specialist (a "shaman") with the power to handle taboo objects, such as leopard remains? And who are the people represented in art donning leopard-skin clothes? Are they perhaps mythical figures living in a time or place where taboos do not apply?

Another interesting example from Çatalhöyük concerns wild boar and pigs. People had been raising domestic pigs in Anatolia for about a millennium before Çatalhöyük was occupied (Price and Hongo, 2020). Moreover, the site was situated within a marshy environment – excellent pig country and an ecological setting in which wild boar would have been common. However, extensive excavations have yielded very few pig or wild boar remains. The relative lack of suid bones in the Çatalhöyük faunal assemblage seems to indicate a conscious decision not to hunt or raise these animals, or at least a strong preference for consuming other species. However, unlike leopards, wild boar remains were not completely absent. The finding of relatively higher ratios of "meaty" skeletal parts (limb, scapula, and pelvis) compared to other parts of the body in the off-site KOPAL area suggests that consumption did occur, at least nearby the settlement (Russell, 2018, p. 20). Meanwhile, skull remains are found in some abundance at the settlement, as are artifacts made from boar tusks (Russell, 2018, p. 23). In one case, a boar head was installed as a wall decoration (Twiss, 2006). Speculating that boar tusks and other parts may have served as markers of social identity, Russell (2018, p. 23) suggests that suids were subject to a partial taboo – taboo to a segment of the population. Alternatively, boar may have been a special food, taboo for most of the year but eaten on special occasions; or perhaps it was a taboo that people occasionally transgressed, particularly in places beyond the immediate confines of the settlement.

Paleolithic Patterns

If detecting and decoding food taboos in prehistory is difficult, it is made even more difficult in most Paleolithic contexts due to the more ephemeral nature (frequent abandonment and re-occupation) and low chronological resolution typical of sites older than c. 10,000 years. If a taboo emerged, flourished, and declined within a 200-year period, and the level of chronological resolution in the stratigraphic sequence is 300 years, one is unlikely to detect the taboo. Ma'ayan Lev and Ran Barkai (2016) nevertheless attempt to push the envelope in their exploration of the possibility of Paleolithic taboos on the meat of proboscideans (the taxonomic order that includes elephants).

Lev and Barkai (2016) argue that the high frequency of taboos on elephant meat among hunter-gatherers today is due to the behavioral similarities between humans and proboscideans, which can promote feelings of kinship. Eating an elephant is, they argue, analogous to cannibalism. Engaging in some healthy, if heavy, speculation, they contemplate whether elephant taboos may have existed in the Paleolithic. The frequent depiction of proboscideans by ancient artists forms a key line of evidence (Lev and Barkai, 2016, p. 243), as does the use of their bones for tools, artwork, and, at the 25,000-year-old Pavlovian sites, construction material (Lev and Barkai, 2016, p. 240). Of course, there is abundant evidence for the hunting of mammoths and mastodons across Eurasia and North America, so the taboo could not have been terribly widespread. Nevertheless, the logic that sympathy between humans and animals (if not exclusively proboscideans) provides the emotional foundation for meat taboos deserves attention, as does the fact that taboos *must* have existed at least in the Upper Paleolithic, even if we cannot readily detect them.

The "Ichth" Factor: A Neolithic Fish Taboo in Northern Europe?

Though they get less attention in archaeology, fish taboos are quite common cross-culturally. Major reasons for the lack of attention are poor preservation of fish remains and low-resolution recovery techniques. In some cases, analysis of stable isotopes from human remains and ceramic residues can help. The biological tissues of marine animals possess a higher ratio of ^{13}C to ^{12}C than those of terrestrial animals (or rather, terrestrial mammals that do not consume marine foods) (e.g., Schoeninger, 2014). In fact, stable isotopic methods lie behind what has become one of the more heated controversies in the archaeology of taboos: whether a taboo on fish and other marine resources developed in the Neolithic of Britain and areas along the North Sea coast.

The Neolithic fish taboo debate kicked off in a paper by Julian Thomas (2003). Thomas relied on carbon isotopic measurements of human bone collagen published by Richards and Hedges (1999), a study that indicated no contribution of marine protein to the diet. This was curious because fish would have offered a valuable source of calories to people living in the region. The lack of fish was, therefore, a conspicuous absence. Thomas, smelling something fishy, raised the specter of a taboo.

Nicky Milner and colleagues (2004) challenged this interpretation. Relying on faunal data – that is, fish bones – they argued that marine exploitation was, in fact, quite prevalent. The isotopic data must be reflecting something else. Their paper could be read as a critique of the validity of isotopic work, and Richards and Schulting (2006) took the bait, countering that although marine exploitation may have existed, it was of minimal dietary importance. People may have eaten a fish here and there, and those bones accumulated in the archaeological record, but Neolithic folk mostly avoided the sea's harvest. After all, isotopes are a more direct reflection of human diet than faunal remains. In their reply to the reply, Milner *et al.* (2006) demurred, arguing that faunal remains reflect long-term dietary trends and are thus a better indicator of food traditions.

What is interesting about this debate is that it wound up being one about methods, rather than interpretation, and in particular whether stable isotopes or faunal remains are more reliable indicators of past diets. For that reason, it holds important lessons for an archaeology of food taboos. Zooarchaeology (nowadays "social zooarchaeology") has long monopolized the study of taboos, but isotopic analysis, lipid-residue analysis, and other methods can also shed light on food taboos. As this debate shows, one issue that an archaeology of taboos will have to reconcile with is that inferences drawn from stable isotopic signatures often do not line up with zooarchaeological data. The contrast between zooarchaeological and isotopic patterns in the Northern European Neolithic appears in other contexts, such as the Titicaca Basin, where limited isotopic evidence for fish consumption (using a compound-specific approach that allows a more accurate picture of protein origin) contrasts with an abundance of ichthyoarchaeological finds (e.g., Miller *et al.*, 2021).

It is important to remember here that different types of archaeological data represent different scales of human behavior and are subject to different types of taphonomic/diagenetic biases and sources of error. Zooarchaeological and stable isotopic data speak to different aspects/scale of human behavior (Makarewicz, 2016). Zooarchaeology analyzes animal bones and teeth (the objects of diet) and tends to reflect longer-term time- and space-averaged behaviors (Lyman, 2003). Stable isotopic indicators of human diet, on the other hand, are assessed on human tissues (the subjects of diet) and tend to reflect more temporally and spatially discrete behaviors (those of a single person). This is especially the case when analysts employ sequential sampling of enamel or dentine, which can reveal episodic dietary trends over the period of dental tissue development. Ideally, an archaeology of food taboos would integrate zooarchaeological, isotopic, and other data types. However, to do so will require attending to the scale and analytical differences within datasets.

Fish Taboos and Technological Loss in Tasmania

Another controversial prehistoric fish taboo concerns Tasmania. Specifically, some have proposed a taboo on fish to explain a curious phenomenon: the cessation of marine exploitation and the loss of fishing technology on the island. Archaeological excavations reveal that fish were an important source of the diet up until around 5,000 years ago; after that point, the relative abundance of fish remains declined. By 3800 BP, fish had disappeared entirely from the diet (Jones, 1995; Henrich, 2004, p. 199). Three and a half millennia later, European visitors, colonists, and ethnographers reported that Indigenous Tasmanians from across the island harbored taboos against scaled fish, although they did consume other marine animals, including shellfish, marine mammals, and seabirds (Jones, 1978, 1984, 1995).

One prominent argument is that Tasmanians developed a taboo as "an intellectual decision which had the result of constricting their ecological universe" (Jones, 1978, pp. 44–45). The taboo, rather than being ecologically or economically adaptive, made subsistence more difficult, according to Rhys Jones, an early proponent of the taboo hypothesis. In essence, Jones reasoned that the taboo on fish, which was documented in the 19th-century ethnohistorical record, extended deep into the past and explains the prehistoric abandonment of fishing. Jones' thesis galvanized discussion and counter-theories (Allen, 1978; Horton, 1979; Bowdler, 1980; Henrich, 2004). Some have even made the case that the cessation of fishing was ecologically adaptive (e.g., Allen, 1978), although that argument has convinced few archaeologists.

The existence of a prehistoric taboo is so controversial because it takes place within the framework of the larger debate surrounding foodways, technology, and cultural evolution. The cessation of fishing, and the tools required for it, went hand-in-hand with a broader decline in technological complexity on the island. Interestingly, Tasmania represents one of the few places around the globe where populations of *Homo sapiens* lost technology. The list is impressive: bone tools, boomerangs, cold-weather clothing, nets, and other technologies that would seem important for subsistence began to disappear around 10,000 years ago. Still more interesting, the loss of technology occurred in the Holocene, a period that witnessed, on the one hand, rapid technological sophistication across the globe, and, on the other, the inundation of the land bridge between continental Australia and Tasmania(Diamond, 1997, pp. 312–313; Henrich, 2004).

The uniqueness of this technological downturn has understandably attracted much interest – after all, the conditions under which technology develops, stagnates, or is lost is one area in which the historical sciences can offer insights that directly affect how we envision and plan for the future. Henrich (2004) has devised a convincing model for demographically mediated technological loss. In his model, low population density, coupled with isolation from other populations, inevitably leads to technological and "maladaptive" loss due to the lowered probability of each generation producing a person possessing the same or greater natural ability to master a particular skill. To give a concrete example, a small population is at a greater risk of not being able to produce a child who can master the production of complex microliths. If that population has no contact with other groups from which to relearn the technology, microlith production techniques are liable to be lost.

If one believes Henrich's (2004) explanation for the cessation of fishing – that it was an outcome of "maladaptive" technological loss for which demographic factors were ultimately responsible – then the origins of the taboo should not be sought in an "intellectual decision" (Jones, 1978, pp. 44–45). Rather, the taboo becomes a consequence of the inability to catch fish due to the failure to pass on the knowledge for fashioning bone fishhooks and nets. The taboo, therefore, would have come about after the technological loss, not as an inspiration for it. It would be an example of a people harboring a taboo on an unfamiliar food source once they came into contact with fish-eating other, especially if that "other" was generally unfriendly. This explanation resonates with the origins of the pig taboo among the Israelites and Jews, described in a subsequent section.

Patagonian Fish Taboo

One final example of hypothetical fish taboos in prehistory demonstrates the power of combining ethnographic and archaeological information. Dánae Fiore and Atilio Francisco J. Zangrando (2006) analyzed the conspicuous absence of Patagonian blennie (*Eleginus maclovinus*) in the 2,000-year archaeological sequence of the Beagle Channel area of Tierra del Fuego. At four archaeological sites, the authors identified only three blennie specimens out of a total of 7,039 identified fish specimens. They argue that this species should be "high-ranking" from a cultural ecological perspective due to its large size and availability (the blennie swims close to the shoreline).

Fiore and Zangrando (2006) interpret this contradiction between expected dietary rank and observed relative abundance with reference to the depiction of various fish species. Specifically, they draw upon photographs and ethnographic descriptions of body painting recorded from the 16th to 20th centuries. In a male initiation ceremony, known as the *kina*, men would dress up as various animals, including Patagonian blennie. (Not all types of fish depicted in the body paint have been securely identified, but all of those with secure or tentative identifications are also relatively rare in the faunal remains.) The *kina* ceremony recounts a myth in which women once dominated men by dressing up as spirits. As the myth goes, men discovered the secret and now are the ones who dress up as spirits and control the women. The authors additionally point out that shoreline fishing was an exclusively female activity. Thus, the authors reason that the blennie was a species ceremonially connected to maleness. It was taboo, they argue, for women to handle it; thus, the blennie was not captured in the female-dominated economic sphere of shoreline fishing.

The Archaeology of Historically Attested Taboos

Taboos in Early Modern Japan

When we know a taboo existed – or was hypothesized to have existed – we can move beyond speculation and test hypotheses. This is where the historical record can come in handy. Rather than confirming preconceived ideas, the results are often surprising. An interesting case study comes from early modern Japan (17th–19th centuries CE). Within the historiography of Japanese foodways is the notion that people abstained from meat, especially from mammals, in this period as a result of the influence of Buddhism (Shimizu, 2010). Making matters tricky, this notion articulates with nationalist beliefs concerning the fundamental differences between Japanese and non-Japanese culture (Krämer, 2008).

Archaeological research has increasingly questioned this taboo, which may have been more of an ideal than a cultural institution – perhaps it was more of a *wertrational* avoidance than a taboo in the strictest sense. Unfortunately for me, much of the literature on the topic is in Japanese (Hitomi Hongo, personal communication). Yet the material published in English provides an example of the power of historical archaeology to analyze food taboos.

In a sweeping article discussing taboos and food preferences among different social strata in Edo period Japan (1603–1868), Jun'ya Sakurai (2017) throws a wrench in the idea that early modern Japanese foodways were meat-free. Buddhist teachings certainly discouraged consuming the killing and eating of four-legged animals, and laws even supported the taboo. In 1688, the state (*bokufu*) issued an edict mandating seventy days of defilement for even physical contact with the corpses of pigs, dogs, and deer, and 150 days for cattle and horses, which were more valuable as draft animals and thus subject to more stringent taboos and punishment (Shimizu, 2010, p. 93). Yet zooarchaeological studies of Japanese sites dating to the Edo period contain the remains of cattle, pig/wild boar, deer (*Cervus nippon*), and other mammals and thus indicate frequent transgression, even among the highest classes.

A critical investigation of historical data also shows that the taboo on mammalian meat may not have been widely practiced. Texts document that the Japanese peasantry was "fond of wild boar meat" and cookbooks from the 18th century include recipes for *butajiro* (a pork-based soup) (Walker, 2001, p. 342). The capital, Edo, itself had two meat markets, which grew towards the end of the period (Shimizu, 2010). In fact, it appears that a culture developed around polite ways of violating the taboo. A common strategy was to claim that the consumption of meat was for medicinal purposes (*kusurigui*), thus avoiding overt transgression (Shimizu, 2010, p. 92). Another tactic was the deployment of colorful pseudonyms for meat (e.g., "maple leaf" for venison or "mountain whale" for wild boar) (Sakurai, 2017, p. 681). The use of such speakeasy terms to avoid mentioning the unmentionable, even in the act of violating the taboo, is something we see in many cultures. "White Steak" is sometimes used in Israeli restaurants as a euphemism for pork (Barak-Erez, 2007, p. 12); semi-clandestine restaurants serving dog meat in Vietnam often advertise it as "fox meat" (Avieli, 2011, p. 59).

It seems likely, therefore, that the extent of the taboos of mammalian meat has been exaggerated in historical texts. Avoiding these animals was an ideal, especially one to which the elite strata strove, or fancied themselves as striving. But it was not a taboo rigorously adhered to. To the extent that taboo was followed, it was in avoiding overt (or perhaps profane) consumption. People accomplished this by shrouding meat-eating in ritual-medicinal practice and punting the taboo on meat consumption to a taboo on *speaking about* meat consumption. It is perhaps not surprising that this taboo, weakly felt as an intuitive belief and poorly followed as a cultural prohibition, did not survive into the later modern period.

Sakurai (2017) examines the archaeological signature of other taboos. One was the consumption of toxic pufferfish (Family Tetraodontidae). Legally, were a family head to die of tetrodotoxin poisoning, the line would be considered socially extinct. Yet remains of pufferfish have been found in middens associated with the residences of lords (*daimyo*) (Sakurai, 2017, p. 681). It would seem, then, that taboo transgression was a regular feature of everyday life, even at the highest levels of society in Edo-period Japan.

Sakurai (2017) also examines the consumption of foods that were not taboo, per se, but considered so low in status as to border on taboo in certain contexts. Tuna offers an interesting case study. Sakurai quotes the 18th-century text *Efu Fuzokushi* ("History of Manners and Customs of Edo District"): "Tuna, sweet potato, pumpkin, and such are exceedingly low-class foods, and even commoners are ashamed to eat them openly" (2017, p. 680). "Shame" is a common reaction to taboo transgression; it also provides fertile soil in which a taboo can germinate. Yet in early modern Japan, the exact opposite happened. Examining one site (referred to only as "the site on the grounds of the Ministry of Posts and Telecommunications Iikura Annex"), on which was situated residential buildings belonging to a *daimyo*, Sakurai reports that the remains of tuna became more common in the 18th century (Sakurai, 2017, pp. 679–680). Whatever anxieties once surrounded this fish relaxed significantly such that the upper echelons of society felt more willing to eat it. This trend continued, as tuna soon became one of the more popular fish in modern Japan and remains a prominent food in Japanese cuisine today (Sakurai, 2017, p. 681).

The examples from early modern Japan provide food for thought on the differences between taboos and other types of prohibitions. It also offers abundant evidence for an important, but often neglected, cultural universal: Transgressions are a regular feature of human existence. Of course, the material signature of transgression complicates detection of taboos, especially in prehistoric archaeology. For historical archaeology, however, it opens up an interesting avenue of cultural interpretation: What are the conditions and contexts under which taboos are broken? Who breaks taboos? On this question, Sakurai draws yet another interesting connection. In the early modern period are found many examples of a unique type of inhumation – "head-covered-with-pot" burials. Sakurai (2017, pp. 688–689) suggests that some of those buried in this manner were recognized by their family or community as transgressors of food taboos and other types of taboos. Others may have suffered from stigmatized illnesses, such as Hansen's Disease. Arguably, the pots served as a sort of protective measure against contaminating the rest of the community with their sins; but if Sakurai is correct, then the pots provide archaeologists another material signature of transgression and its prevalence.

Horsemeat in Europe

Another example of a historically attested taboo is that on horsemeat in parts of medieval and modern Europe. Prior to the mid-late medieval period, especially in the 1st millennium AD, consumption of horses was not unusual in Britain and across Europe. Pope Gregory III banned the practice in 732 (Wilson and Edwards, 1993, p. 51), and the Church in Rome increasingly sought to eliminate the practice, which it associated with paganism (Poole, 2013). Even still, horsemeat was a regular food in eastern Europe and the Eurasian Steppe (Simoons, 1994, p. 183) and people continued to eat horses in Denmark and Ireland, at least occasionally, despite the ban (Simoons, 1994, p. 188).

The archaeological record includes examples of butchered horse remains that can present archaeologists with interpretational difficulties. For example, in one deposit at Witney Palace in Oxfordshire, UK, dating to the 18th century CE, horse bones represented over 95 percent of the recovered fragments (Wilson and Edwards, 1993). The remains were found in a deposit adjacent to the palace buildings. Most of these horses died in their prime, aged four to nine years (Wilson and Edwards, 1993, p. 47). However, the authors argue that horsemeat was *not* part of human diet, on the basis of historical evidence and the fact that the deposit was so dominated by horse remains and not that of other livestock. Instead, they suggest the horses were butchered for feeding dogs and for their skins.

The argument that the Witney Palace horse remains reflect carcass use for reasons other than human consumption is sound. After all, the use of horsehides and horsemeat for feeding dogs are historically attested (Wilson and Edwards, 1993, p. 51). But one could argue that it represents a convenient explanation by archaeologists either unwilling to face taboo transgression in the past or worried that such an argument would appear to be sensational. One is left with the nagging question: How would one differentiate the consumption of horses by humans from the consumption of horses by dogs? One potential indicator of consumption by dogs would be evidence for gnawing on horse remains; while evidence for consumption by humans could be indicated by burning or other cooking marks. Interestingly, evidence for gnawing was rather uncommon, but burning was entirely absent (Wilson and Edwards, 1993, p. 47).

While there is no good reason to doubt the conclusions drawn about the Witney Palace horses, archaeologists should not be reluctant to admit the possibility that butchered horse remains reflect dietary usage. There is historical evidence for eating horsemeat, especially during famines and sieges (Simoons, 1994, pp. 188–189). Archaeologists have also noted the presence of butchered horse remains in a variety of European and colonial contexts, which suggest occasional consumption of equines in certain settings (Smith, 1999; Pavao-Zuckerman *et al.*, 2018).

As a bit of a historical sidenote, the horse taboo in Europe offers an example of a conscious attempt to lift a prohibition via the application of Weberian *Zweckrationalität*. The effort, variously successful, stemmed, in part, from the same type of Victorian-era modernism that inspired early anthropologists to examine the concept of taboo critically. It involved, in the language of Sperber (1997), the confrontation of intuitive beliefs about the non-food-ness of horses with the reflective belief that horsemeat is as edible as that of any other animal. Crippling poverty in the early modern period also played a role; it was after the discovery that the French poor, who had been eating horses as a source of cheap meat, suffered no health effects that arguments in favor of "hippophagy" gained traction (Weil, 2007). France was the scene of the most successful lifting of this taboo, in no small part due to the proselytizing of the French military veterinarian, Émile Decroix (1821–1901). Decroix argued, quite reasonably, that refusing to eat horsemeat was wasteful, especially if so many of the poor in France were going without meat. Moreover, if horses were sold for their meat, their owners would be incentivized to keep them in good condition – and not abuse their animals (Weil, 2007, p. 46).

Decroix's ideas gained some traction and horsemeat continues to be eaten in France to this day, though not without occasional protest. The attempt to lift the taboo was less successful in other countries. In 1868, horsemeat banquets were held in England, as they were in France (Simoons, 1994, p. 190). But the taboo proved harder to lift. In 2013, there was a scandal in the UK and Europe when DNA revealed horsemeat in many products sold as beef (Lawrence, 2013).

Haram *Meat in the Swahili World*

Islam is a global religion with over one billion adherents, most of whom profess to avoiding forbidden (*haram*) foods as part of their religious practice. But, as is the case with all taboos, violation is not uncommon. An interesting example derives from archaeological investigations in the Swahili culture of the East African Coast. Social complexity rapidly emerged in this region by the end of the 1st millennium CE, with urban-sized settlements of up to 20,000 people (Kusimba, 2023). By the early 2nd millennium CE, Swahili-speaking elites and the stone towns from which they ruled sat at the southwestern edge of an exchange system that stretched across the Indian Ocean and on to China and was visited by famous travelers such as Ibn Battuta and Zheng He. Islam appeared on the coast at the same time that urbanism began to flourish, with the first mosques dating to the 8th century (Horton, 1996). Widespread conversion to Islam occurred around the 14th century, and Islam would remain a key feature of Swahili society up to the present day (Kusimba, 2023).

The dietary taboos in Islam derive from the *Quran*, *hadiths*, and their interpretations. They include the well-known taboo on pork, which is spelled out in the Quran. Depending on which scholarly interpretations one follows, restrictions also apply to other animals relevant to Swahili foodways, such as sea turtles and dugongs. Yet all these animals have been found at various Swahili sites, including within elite and non-elite houses, tombs, and, most intriguingly, in mosques. These bones, though not very common, often display signs of consumption such as cut marks and burning (Boivin *et al.*, 2014, p. 560).

Finds of these *haram* animals raise intriguing questions regarding Islamic practice and its negotiations. Do they represent the persistence of non-Muslim traditions? Or perhaps a rejection of certain Muslim tenets? How were those who violated the taboos perceived? Chaparukha Kusimba (personal communication) has witnessed the consumption of sea turtle and dugong during the course of ethnographic investigation into foodways of Muslim and non-Muslim households in the Lamu archipelago. In these cases, animals were eaten clandestinely, as they may have been in the past. Yet the role of these animals in archaeological contexts related to ritual raises the possibility that consumption in the past was conspicuous and charged – that the consumption of *haram* meat may have been a powerful feature of the ritual activity. Rituals, after all, are often the only appropriate context in which to violate a taboo.

The Pig Taboo

The pig taboo in Judaism and Islam has garnered much attention from archaeologists, historians, theologians, and other commentators. The taboo, though one of many included in Leviticus, is among the most emotionally charged avoidance practices that create a sense of self-identity among Jews. Adopted by Islam in the 7th century and some Christian denominations (e.g., Ethiopian Orthodox), it is now followed by well over a billion people worldwide. Within Europe, it separated Christians from Jews and Muslims, thus becoming almost metonymic of ethnoreligious identity (Price, 2021, pp. 184–189; Rosenblum, 2024).

People have tried to understand the pig taboo for millennia. The earliest attempts to do so can actually be found in its biblical codification. The first written attestation of the taboo appears in the Book of Leviticus (Leviticus 11.7) alongside a reason for it rooted in animal physiology (pigs have cloven hoofs but do not ruminate, the biblical authors explained). Roman writers also speculated on its origins, oftentimes mixing explanation with anti-Jewish insults. For example, Tacitus (AD 56–117) claimed that Moses invented the food laws to gain power over his people and to oppose the traditions of other peoples; he also claimed that a skin disease contracted from pigs once afflicted the Jews (*Histories* 5.4).

Anthropological interest in the pig taboo is almost as old as the discipline. As discussed in Section 2, it has long served as a point of reference for the taboos of other cultures (Frazer, 1912; Simoons, 1961; Douglas, 1966; Harris, 1985b). The pig taboo has found itself used in support of more sweeping theories concerning the nature and significance of taboos. For example, when Carleton Coon (1951, p. 346) and Marvin Harris (1985b) argued that the pig taboo was an adaptation to the environment of the Levant, they implied that the taboo was first a *zweckrational* proscription imposed by an ecologically conscious elite. On the other hand, Mary Douglas' (1966) argument that the pork taboo reflects a fear of "dangerous" mixtures, or Milgrom's (1998) contention that pigs were redolent of death and thus made taboo, tend to fall back on the kind of magical thinking that draws power from associational thought.

Within archaeology, no taboo has received more attention. In large part, this is because of the magnitude of biblical archaeology and longstanding scholarly and lay interest in the historicity of the Hebrew Bible. The pig taboo has become a focal point in the debates concerning the origins and identification of the Israelite people (Hesse and Wapnish, 1998, 2000; Lev-Tov, 2000; Horwitz *et al.*, 2017; Faust, 2018; Sapir-Hen, 2018; Fulton, 2020; Greer, 2020; Price, 2021). I cannot review all of this literature here, but I have written at length on the topic in a previous book (Price, 2021) and can summarize my main arguments: First, the pig taboo's origins are obscure but can be traced to multiple causes that coalesced in the early part of the Iron Age, which lasted from around 1200–330 BC. Second – and a point missed by many archaeologists and anthropologists – the pig taboo as we know it in Judaism or Islam today is not the same as that practiced in the Iron Age. The pig taboo *evolved*, its meaning changing over time as it became a signifier of identity in different cultural and political contexts.

One should approach the origins of the pig taboo in the long and complex history of pigs in Middle Eastern political economies, cultural dynamics, and religious thought. Among the four mammalian livestock species domesticated in the Neolithic (the others being sheep, goats, and cattle), pigs always stood apart: They are multiparous, omnivorous, and less socially gregarious than the ruminants. They provided no valuable "secondary products," such as wool or traction power, that could be turned into commodities for long-distance exchange or harnessed to increase the productive capabilities of human labor. As such, pigs possessed quite different types of value (use value, exchange value, and symbolic value) than the ruminants (Price, 2021, pp. 64–67).

I have hypothesized that the difference in value between pigs and animals explains a curious and currently not-well-understood pattern: Zooarchaeological data indicate that pig husbandry gradually disappeared in the Levant in the 3rd through 2nd Millennia BC, centuries before the Bible was composed. While people in other parts of the Middle East (especially Egypt and Mesopotamia) continued to raise pigs, often in large numbers, it is almost certainly not a coincidence that pigs vanished from the very region in which the famous taboo would later develop (Price, 2021, pp. 73–75). Pigs were not so much avoided in the Bronze Age, but other animals were more alluring. If I am right, then this *passive* nonconsumption of pork – and not a taboo – ultimately evolved into a unique feature of Levantine food traditions. Avoidance of pork became increasingly active and conscious during the Iron Age (1200–330 BC).

Much debate has swirled around whether pigs played a role in the ethnogenesis of Israelites and Philistines, the latter having ancestry from the Aegean region. It is too simplistic to argue that "Philistines = pork-eaters and Israelites = pork-haters" (Hesse and Wapnish, 2000; Fulton, 2020), but the fact remains that urban sites associated with Philistine material culture, such as Tel es-Safi and Tel Miqne, contain 10–20 percent pig remains (by NISP) in the 12th–10th centuries BC, while almost no pig remains were found at nearby cities dominated by Israelite material culture, such as Lachish, which was less than 20 km away (Lev-Tov, 2000, 2012; Vermeersch et al., 2021). It is hard to explain this difference other than as what Fowles (2008) would call a "conspicuous absence." It also parallels other material differences in foodways (e.g., cooking ware, ceramic types, plant foods, spices) between Philistines and local Israelite/Canaanite peoples (see Price, 2022). There must have been conscious awareness of the differences in diet; foodways are commonly used by people to self-identify and to identify others (Hastorf, 2016; Twiss, 2019).

The question is: How important was pork avoidance in the self-identification among Israelites? It may not have been as important as some assume (e.g., Faust, 2018). Or it may have faded in importance over time. In any event, pig consumption was not totally absent at Israelite sites, especially in the northern kingdom of Israel beginning in the 8th century BC (Sapir-Hen et al., 2013; Sapir-Hen, 2018). The fact that the biblical texts were written in or by people identifying with the southern kingdom of Judah sometime after the 8th century may reflect regional differences in Israelite culture.

Whatever the nature of the pig taboo early on, it was eventually inscribed by the biblical writers (people connected with the priesthood of Judah) into the Book of Leviticus. It was one proscription of *many* against "impure" (Hebrew: *tameh*) foods. There is no consensus on when the biblical passages against pigs were written down (authors "P" and "H"), with estimates ranging from the 8th through 5th centuries BC (Milgrom, 1998, pp. 3–30; Coogan, 2017; Rhyder, 2021). But whoever and whenever they were, the biblical writers apparently felt compelled to explain the taboo, which they did by reference to pigs' physiology, namely their lack of rumination and presence of cloven hooves. Mary Douglas (1966) famously made much of this explanation in her exploration of taboos and dangerous mixtures. But it is far more likely that the physiological explanation found in Leviticus is a post-facto rationalization for an existing taboo that, like all taboos, is primarily felt on an emotional level rather than reasoned on a rational level. In the case of the biblical writers, it is not too difficult to imagine that the biblical writers were attempting to frame the prohibition with reference to the essential characteristic inscribed in animals by a creator deity (Price, 2021, p. 133).

Textual and historical evidence, backed up by zooarchaeology (complete lack of pig bones at sites associated with Jewish communities in contrast to relatively high numbers at non-Jewish settlements), indicates that the pig taboo evolved over the next several centuries as pork-avoidance became a more salient indication of Jewishness. It did so in the context of conquest, colonization, and rule by the pork-eating (and loving) peoples of the Greek and Roman world (Rosenblum, 2010; Rhyder, 2023). In the Roman period, in particular, pork became caught in a dialectic between the ideological and political spheres of Hellenism and Judaism, as Roman satirists poked fun at the Jewish taboo and early rabbis made pigs representative of everything evil about Rome – its apparent (or material) prosperity coming at the expense of its spiritual poverty and moral bankruptcy (Rosenblum, 2024). At the same time, Greek colonists and Roman legionaries settled in the Levant, bringing with them their love of pork and sometimes even using pigs in rituals (Perry-Gal *et al.*, 2022; Perry-Gal, Lieberman, and Uziel, 2024). At this point, pork consumption truly became the food taboo *par excellence* of the Jewish people, surpassing the dozens of other food taboos in Leviticus in importance.

Interestingly, and in passing, there has been relatively little discussion of the other taboos in Leviticus. The biblical authors, after all, prohibited not just pigs, but also any non-ruminating or non-cloven-hoofed mammal, fish without scales and fins, and various birds (Altmann and Spiciarich, 2020). Also taboo were animals that "creep" on the ground (Hebrew: *sheratzim*). Thus, in a few lines, Leviticus made off-limits the meat of many animals enjoyed in other cultures: rabbit, lobster, camel, shellfish, catfish, dogs, horses, guinea pigs, and eels, to name a few. These "other" animals are technically no less taboo than pigs, according to the Bible.

There has been some attempt to examine these taboos in the Iron Age. For example, catfish bones are found in high relative abundance in archaeological contexts through the Persian period, possibly suggesting that this taboo was not followed by the majority of Israelites/Jews until the Hellenistic/Roman period (Adler and Lernau, 2021) – the same time when the pig taboo appears to have become more significant. In general, however, more work needs to be done on the zooarchaeology of these "other" Leviticus food taboos.

The archaeology of the pig taboo falls somewhat in between prehistoric and historical archaeology. It is historically attested, but the most salient periods for its emergence (the 12th–10th centuries BC) are largely lacking in texts, at least in the southern Levant. Archaeologists have tended to rely on a backward projection of the pig taboo into the earlier parts of the Iron Age, using fragment count (NISP) data from rather small faunal assemblages to argue for or against "conspicuous absences" of pigs. This is a potentially dangerous game, as it can (and does) lead to anachronism. Ultimately, the origins of the pig taboo will remain a mystery for some time, though it almost certainly relates to the dietary drop-off of pork in the Bronze Age Levant and the development of a traditional Levantine foodway that did not include much or any pork.

Archaeologists are on firmer ground in more historically documented periods. Analysis of these contexts has revealed many interesting patterns concerning the evolution of the taboo. The pork taboo "came of age" in the Roman period. It was at this time that it was elevated to something more than one of many food prohibitions and became intimately tied to Jewish identity. But the taboo has continued to evolve in meaning, as archaeologists studying later periods have discovered.

Chosen Taboos

The earliest origins of the pig taboo are contentious, but the adherence to the proscriptions laid out in the Book of Leviticus, and repeated for good measure in Deuteronomy, defined Jewish communities in the Levant and Diaspora for centuries. Because of their distinctive diet, often differing from that of dominant non-Jewish communities, Jewish households can leave identifiable zooarchaeological signatures. Alongside artifactual data, especially Judaica (e.g., menorah), faunal remains can assist in the reconstruction of ethnoreligious maps of historical sites (Valenzuela-Lamas *et al.*, 2014; Lisowski, 2019). Unsurprisingly, the zooarchaeological data are rarely "pure," with pig bones sometimes appearing in "Jewish" contexts. In some of these cases, zooarchaeologists have good reason to suspect transgressions of the food taboos (for review, see Lisowski, 2019, pp. 25–30).

A groundbreaking study of the observance and occasional violation of the biblical food laws among Jewish communities is F. Gerard Ijzereef's (1989) analysis of a large assemblage (>100,000 faunal specimens) of animal remains from 17th- to 18th-century Amsterdam. Most of the animal bones came from cesspits located in the Waterlooplein district, where a community of Portuguese Jews settled around 1600 (and which remained the Jewish Quarter until its liquidation in World War II). As the cesspits were used to dump everyday waste, the contexts were ideal for studying household consumption patterns. Furthermore, the excavation protocols enabled high-resolution analysis. The archaeologists were able to define internal stratigraphical breaks within the cesspits that allowed dating in c. 25-year chunks. They sieved the deposits to increase the recovery rates of faunal remains and other finds. Finally, using historical maps, the archaeologists were able to associate many of the cesspits directly with individual houses, allowing a diachronic house-by-house assessment of diet.

Ijzereef's (1989) analysis divided Jewish from non-Jewish houses on the basis of historical data and, when those were not present, the relative abundance of pig remains. Cesspits with more than 5 percent pigs were considered to be non-Jewish. Any cesspit with less than 1 percent pigs was considered Jewish (or rather kosher-abiding), with fractions of percentages assumed to be contamination or the occasional dumping of waste from another household. These pig-free cesspits also lacked evidence for the hindlimbs of ruminants, which are often avoided because of the taboo on consuming the sciatic nerve (Hebrew: *gid hanasheh*), and the bones of eel and shellfish, which are banned (Leviticus 11:9). The relative abundance of pig remains in non-Jewish households was much higher, around 20–30 percent.

In some case, the historical and zooarchaeological data appeared to conflict. For example, several houses had between 1 and 5 percent pigs. This was quite low for the typical non-Jewish Amsterdammer, but higher than Ijzereef's cutoff for Jewish households. One particularly interesting case concerned a wealthy Jewish household, the cesspits of which contained small numbers of shellfish, rabbit, and lobster – all banned. Ijzereef interpreted these as non-kosher Jewish households or households containing a mix of Jews and non-Jews. However, unless there were separate kitchens and eating areas, the inclusion of non-kosher-eating people in the same household would be a problem, since most Rabbinic commentators caution against cross-contamination. One wonders if perhaps these households, especially the wealthy one, were using food to position themselves more prominently with their gentile neighbors.

The Amsterdam material documents the intersection of class, taboo, and transgression. Another interesting context in which to explore these features is in pioneer settings. In particular, Jews in the so-called "New World" often found themselves in social contexts disconnected from traditional networks. This had an impact on taboo observance and food choice. Scott (1996) analyzed faunal from an 18th-century site in northern Michigan called Fort Michilimackinac, which was captured by the British in 1760 and abandoned in 1781. Scott's analysis focused on the faunal remains recovered from the vicinity of four households living at the fort during these two decades. Like Ijzereef (1989), Scott was able to lean on historical records to inform her analysis. For example, House C, as it was deemed by the archaeologists, was identified as a house purchased in 1765 by two Jewish traders, Ezekiel Solomon and Gershon Levy. Records show that the traders lived in the house until the abandonment of the settlement.

Were Solomon and Levy living in the 21st century, they would probably join a Reform synagogue with a guitar-strumming rabbi. But the Reform movement did not exist in their time. In the 18th century, they were simply "bad Jews." The records from Ezekial Solomon, for example, betray a willingness to bend the rules in this pioneer context. Solomon likely considered himself a Jew; his non-Jewish neighbors at Michilimackinac certainly did. However, he married a French-Canadian woman in 1769, violating the laws against intermarriage (e.g., Deuteronomy 23:4, Nehemiah 10:31), left his sons uncircumcised, and baptized his children (Scott, 1996, p. 370). This may have been part of a desire to fit in, particularly in the context of anti-Semitism (Scott, 1996, p. 370).

The faunal remains from House C, a mix of those produced by Solomon and Levy, offer material evidence of a lax interpretation of Jewish practice. Calculated on the basis of biomass, 13 percent of the faunal remains from House C were from pigs. Scott (1996, p. 365) also identified a smorgasbord of other non-kosher delights, such as squirrel, beaver, rabbit, and sturgeon.

The faunal record from the Michilimackinac site sheds light on the contexts in which people might violate taboos. Scott (1996, p. 370) argues that Solomon and Levy would have faced anti-Semitism and speculates that their consumption of non-kosher foods was an attempt at fitting it. Life on what, for Europeans, was the wild frontier may also have contributed to a sense that the rules of *halakha* could be suspended. Although Scott provides little information on Levy, Solomon appears to have undergone a personal evolution of sorts. The zooarchaeological data indicate he radically cut back on the amount of non-kosher food in his household in the 1770s. His was not a kosher household by any stretch of the imagination, but it was marked by less frequent transgression. These dietary changes coincided with him becoming a more active member of the Jewish community in Montreal, which by that point served as his main residence; Michilimackinac being his summer home.

Scott (1996) attributes the change in Solomon's diet to his increasing wealth. However, one cannot escape the feeling that, like many nonobservant Jews today, he became more spiritually inclined and tradition-bound as he grew older. The case is an excellent example of the ways in which archaeology can, when armed with high-resolution historical data, reveal how individuals change over time, and how taboo adherence or transgression map onto other factors (racism/anti-Semitism, growing older, changing social conditions).

7 Conclusion

Defining Food Taboos and Placing Them on the Archaeologist's Table

The word "taboo" derives from a Polynesian concept that articulates with notions of political power and charisma (*mana*), gender, magic, health anxieties, and a cosmological sense of rightness and wrongness. To the members and readers of Cook's expeditions, the concept offered a way to describe a certain type of avoidance behavior that was more emotional than rational, more felt than reasoned. Though these pre-Boasian thinkers had many faults, and though they often succumbed to the ethnocentrism and racism of their times, one can give them credit for recognizing that taboos were a universal phenomenon. Taboos are a part of the human condition.

That said, the concept of taboo is an abstraction. Because the particularities of taboos differ from context to context, it can be complicated to define and understand this phenomenon. I have argued that taboos are neither *wertrational* (actions reasoned from a moral first principle) or *zweckrational* (actions reasoned from a practical goal), although it is possible that some taboos have their origins in these types of rational thought, prior to becoming enfolded by feelings and instinctiveness and then ferried into the realm of taboos. More relevant to taboos are Weber's (2019) two other factors in determining social action: emotion and tradition. The latter hallows taboos, the former energizes them. Taboos are what Dan Sperber (1997) calls "intuitive beliefs." As Freud (2020) recognized, there is a kinship between the emotions that surround taboos and those that surround contamination obsessions in people suffering from OCD. While the key difference is that taboos are social while obsessions/phobias are personal, it is the emotionality that gives both taboos and obsessions their strength.

Admittedly people follow restrictions for rational reasons *and* emotional reasons, but when an avoidance behavior is more rationally followed than emotionally, it can be argued not to be a taboo. Certainly, when a taboo begins to be subjected more to rational thought, it can lose its power. This might explain why the zooarchaeological record of early modern Japan is so full of butchered animal remains, despite the injunction against the meat of land mammals. It may have been more a Buddhist-inspired *wertrational* avoidance than a taboo in the strictest of senses. Similarly, the frequent consumption of pork by many Jews today, and the lifting of the Biblical prohibitions on food laws by the Reform Movement, are examples of taboos fading in response to rational thought.

Many anthropologists and archaeologists have attempted to construe taboos as functional. They argue taboos are, at least from an evolutionary perspective, *zweckrational*. While, again, there may well have been rational reasons for a taboo to develop, and while behavior can have unanticipated positive or negative effects, I think it is a mistake to approach taboos through this lens. Just as it would miss the point to describe the social imperative for Jews and Muslims to circumcise their sons with respect to the fact that circumcision can lower the risk of transmitting HIV, I think it is a mistake to frame Fijian food taboos around the risks posed by fish poisoning to developing fetuses (Henrich and Henrich, 2010). While the biomedical implications are correct, they are not the reason people follow the taboo, nor do they shed light on the cultural structures that support and are supported by taboos. To mention but one dimension, taboos are intertwined with power and the maintenance of boundaries between social identities. This is why taboos are so often gendered or determined by ethnic affiliation.

The archaeology of food taboos, as I have argued, is essential for the simple reason that taboos are a universal and important part of the human condition, one that influences social structure and, of course, diet. An archaeology that discounts them restricts our ability to comprehend or even appreciate the tapestry of past foodways. The good news is that food taboos, compared to other types of taboos (for example, injunctions against speech or sex acts), are available for study, since so much of the archaeological record reflects the material remains of food production, storage, preparation, consumption, and disposal. However, there are methodological challenges. The disciplinary allergy to deriving meaningful interpretations from "absence of evidence" is among the greatest epistemological hurdles (Fowles, 2008). Another is the unwillingness to speculate – that hesitancy is usually a plus in the social sciences, but in this case, it limits the potential of archaeological interpretation.

Invigorating the Archaeology of Food Taboos

Outside of the extensive literature and resulting debates surrounding cases of cannibalism, the archaeology of food taboos remains in its infancy. While there is more of a willingness to engage in informed speculation, particularly in the past twenty years, there has been little progress on the methodological and theoretical issues as they pertain to archaeological investigation since Fowles (2008) and Russell (2012). Moreover, although archaeological science has arguably undergone a revolution in the past two decades, traditional zooarchaeological techniques have predominated in the study of food taboos.

Within zooarchaeology, analyses of taboo focus on fragment counts (NISP) and estimates of minimum numbers of individuals (MNI); to a lesser extent, analysts have employed spatial analyses of body part representation and butchery patterns. Thus, by and large, it is zooarchaeologists using traditional methodological tools who navigate the seas of food taboos in the past. There are good reasons for this – after all, bones are well represented in the archaeological record, and most food taboos apply to meat – but work needs to be done to increase inter-disciplinarity. One issue that future work on archaeologies of taboo will have to grapple with is how to combine these methodologies in a coherent fashion. As we saw with the hypothetical Neolithic European taboo on marine foods, the addition of new lines of evidence from different methodologies can provide contradictory results. Another issue is the misinterpretation of zooarchaeological data by non-specialists, who may not be aware of the methodological issues pertaining to site formation processes, taphonomic factors, and variable recovery that affect faunal datasets (see Price, 2022).

As the examples show, historical archaeologists are well-positioned to undertake an archaeology of food taboos, for unlike prehistorians, they work in contexts in which taboos are known to have existed. They can work *deductively*. That is, they can use the textual record not as a guide, per se, to the archaeological record, but as a set of hypotheses to be tested. For archaeologists working without the benefit of a relevant textual or ethnographic record, a deductive approach is more elusive. It is possible only to the extent that one can hypothesize that a taboo known from historical or ethnographic data existed in the deep past (e.g., the Tasmanian fish taboo or the pig taboo among early Israelites). Instead, they often work inductively by attempting to find taboos where the faunal record does not match functionalist expectations. This is simply a repackaging of the notion that non-functional behaviors must be ritual.

Historical archaeology offers additional benefits. As the examples here have shown, one of the interesting parts of an archaeology of food taboos is not so much the *detection* of them, but rather the nuances in context in which they apply and are violated. Ethnoarchaeological research is also quite interesting in this regard. Here, the work of Gustavo Politis (Politis and Saunders, 2002; Politis, 2007) among the Nukak stands out. Ethnoarchaeology offers a rare opportunity to study contemporary taboos and the contexts in which transgression occurs.

It is here that analysts should heed caution. In historical and ethnographic settings, uncovering instances of taboo violation may be politically sensitive endeavour, to put it mildly. Taboos reflect deeply held intuitive beliefs that articulate with a sense of right and wrong. Presenting evidence of transgression can pose difficult questions to people regarding their ancestors. It can challenge their sense of identity and, by extension, sense of self. Revealing taboo violation among present-day people can jeopardize the immediate safety of individuals and communities; there is potential for similar risks to descendant communities of archaeological investigations into taboos. These are not trivial issues, but ones that touch upon some of the stickiest ethical questions in our discipline. Should an archaeology of food or other taboos take off in the way that I advocate here, professional societies and granting agencies must adopt a set of regulations to prevent this important work from causing harm.

References

Adler, Y. and Lernau, O. (2021) "The Pentateuchal Dietary Proscription against Finless and Scaleless Aquatic Species in Light of Ancient Fish Remains," *Tel Aviv*. Taylor & Francis, 48(1), pp. 5–26.

Akimichi, T. (1998) "Pig and Man in Papuan Societies: Two Cases from the Seltaman of the Fringe Highlands and the Gidra of the Lowland," *Senri Ethnological Studies*, 47, pp. 163–182.

Allan, K. and Burridge, K. (2006) *Forbidden Words: Taboo and the Censoring of Language*. Cambridge: Cambridge University Press.

Allen, H. (1978) "Left Out in the Cold: Why Tasmanians Stopped Eating Fish," *The Artefact*, 4, pp. 1–10.

Altmann, P., Angelini, A., and Spiciarich, A. (2020) "Introduction," in Altmann, P., Angelini, A., and Spiciarich, A. (eds) *Food Taboos and Biblical Prohibitions: Reassessing Archaeological and Literary Perspectives*. Tübingen: Mohr Siebeck, pp. 1–8.

Altmann, P. and Spiciarich, A. (2020) "Chickens, Partridges, and the/tor/of Ancient Israel and the Hebrew Bible," *Die Welt des Orients*. Vandenhoeck & Ruprecht GmbH & Co. KG Göttingen, 50(1), pp. 2–30.

Avieli, N. (2011) "Dog Meat Politics in a Vietnamese Town," *Ethnology*, 50, pp. 59–78.

Barak-Erez, D. (2007) *Outlawed Pigs: Law, Religion, and Culture in Israel*. Madison: University of Wisconsin Press.

Beaglehole, J. C. (ed.) (1967) *The Journals of Captain James Cook on His Voyages of Discovery: Volume III Part Two*. New York: Cambridge University Press.

Beaty, R. E. and Kenett, Y. N. (2023) "Associative Thinking at the Core of Creativity," *Trends in Cognitive Sciences*. Elsevier, 27, pp. 671–683.

Van den Berghe, P. L. (1980) "Incest and Exogamy: A Sociobiological Reconsideration," *Ethology and Sociobiology*. Elsevier, 1(2), pp. 151–162.

Boivin, N., Crowther, A., Prendergast, M. and Fuller, D. Q. (2014). Indian Ocean food globalisation and Africa. *African Archaeological Review*, 31, 547–581.

Bonomo, M. and Politis, G. (2021) "Humanized Nature: Symbolic Representation of Fauna in Pottery from the Paraná River of South America," in Bonomo, M. and Archila, S. (eds) *South American Contributions to World Archaeology*. Cham: Springer Nature, pp. 411–446.

Bowdler, S. (1980) "Fish and Culture: A Tasmanian polemic," *The Australian Journal of Anthropology*. Sydney University Press for the Anthropological Society of New South Wales., 12: 334–340.

Bray, T. L. (2003) "The Commensal Politics of Early States and Empires," in Bray, T. L. (ed.) *The Archaeology and Politics of Food and Feasting in Early States and Empires*. New York: Kluwer Academic, pp. 1–13.

Burke, E. (2015) "An Appeal from the New to the Old Whigs," in Marshall, P. J., Bryant, D. C., and Todd, W. B. (eds) *The Writings and Speeches of Edmund Burke, Vol. 4: Party, Parliament, and the Dividing of the Whigs: 1780–1794*. Oxford: Oxford University Press, pp. 365–477.

Caplan, P. (2008) "Crossing the Veg/Non-veg Divide: Commensality and Sociality among the Middle Classes in Madras/Chennai," *South Asia: Journal of South Asian Studies*. Taylor & Francis, 31(1), pp. 118–142.

Coogan, M. D. (2017) *The Old Testament: A Historical and Literary Introduction to the Hebrew Scriptures, 4th Ed.* Oxford: Oxford University Press.

Coon, C. S. (1951) *Caravan: The Story of the Middle East*. New York: Henry Holt.

DeBoer, W. R. (1987) "You Are What You Don't Eat: Yet Another Look at Food Taboos in Amazonia," in Auger, R., Glass, M. E, MacEachern, S., and McCartney, P. H. (eds) *Ethnicity and Culture*. Calgary: The University of Calgary Press, pp. 45–54.

Diamond, J. (1997) *Guns, Germs, and Steel: The Fate of Human Societies*. New York: W. W. Norton.

Diener, P. and Robkin, E. E. (1978) "Ecology, Evolution, and the Search for Cultural Origins: The Question of Islamic Pig Prohibition," *Current Anthropology*, 19(2), pp. 493–540.

Dietler, M. (2001) "Theorizing the Feast: Rituals of Consumption, Commensal Politics, and Power in African Contexts," in Dietler, M. and Hayden, B. (eds) *Feasts: Archaeological and Ethnographic Perspectives on Food, Politics, and Power*. Washington, DC: Smithsonian Institute Press, pp. 65–114.

Douglas, M. (1966) *Purity and Danger: An Analysis of Concepts of Pollution and Taboo*. London: Routledge and Kegan Paul.

Douglas, M. (1975) *Implicit Meanings: Essays in Anthropology*. London: Routledge and Kegan Paul.

Douglas, M. (2000) "Deep Thoughts on the Forbidden," *Science*, 289, p. 2288.

Douglas, M. (2002) *Purity and Danger: An Analysis of Concepts of Pollution and Taboo*. New York: Routledge Classics.

Durkheim, E. (1995) *The Elementary Forms of the Religious Life*. New York: The Free Press.

Faust, A. (2018) "Pigs in Space (and Time) Pork Consumption and Identity Negotiations in the Late Bronze and Iron Ages of Ancient Israel," *Near Eastern Archaeology*, 81, pp. 276–299.

Fessler, D. M. T. and Navarrete, C. D. (2003) "Meat Is Good to Taboo: Dietary Proscriptions as a Product of the Interaction of Psychological Mechanisms and Social Processes," *Journal of Cognition and Culture*, 3, pp. 1–40.

Fiddes, N. (1991) *Meat: A Natural Symbol*. New York: Routledge.

Fiore, D. and Zangrando, A. F. J. (2006) "Painted Fish, Eaten Fish: Artistic and Archaeofaunal Representations in Tierra del Fuego, Southern South America," *Journal of Anthropological Archaeology*. Elsevier, 25(3), pp. 371–389.

Fitzpatrick, K. K. (2018) "Foraging and Menstruation in the Hadza of Tanzania. Unpublished PhD Dissertation. Department of Archaeology & Anthropology University of Cambridge.

Fowles, S. (2008) "Steps toward an Archaeology of Taboo," in Fogelin, L. (ed.) *Religion, Archaeology, and the Material World*. Carbondale: Southern Illinois University. Center for Archaeological Investigations, Occasional Paper No. 36, pp. 15–37.

Frazer, J. G. (1886) "Taboo," *Encyclopedia Britannica, 9th Ed, vol. XXIII*.

Frazer, J. G. (1911) *The Golden Bough: A Study in Magic and Religion. Volume 3: Taboo and the Perils of the Soul*. London: MacMillan.

Frazer, J. G. (1912) *The Golden Bough: A Study in Magic and Religion. Volume 8: Spirits of the Corn and of the Wild (Part 2)*. London: MacMillan.

Freud, S. (2020) *Totem and Taboo: Resemblances between the Psychic Lives of Savages and Neurotics*. Warsaw: Ktoczyta.pl.

Fu, J. and Altmann, P. (2014) "Feasting: Backgrounds, Theoretical Perspectives, and Introductions," in Altmann, P. and Fu, J. (eds) *Feasting in the Archaeology and Texts of the Bible and the Ancient Near East*. Winona Lake (IN): Eisenbrauns, pp. 1–31.

Fulton, D. N. (2020) "Distinguishing Judah and Philistia: A Zooarchaeological View from Ramat Raḥel and Ashkelon," in Altmann, P., Angelini, A., and Spiciarich, A. (eds) *Food Taboos and Biblical Prohibitions: Reassessing Archaeological and Literary Perspectives*. Tübingen: Mohr Siebeck, pp. 87–106.

Gell, A. (1979) "Reflections on a Cut Finger: Taboo in the Umeda Conception of the Self," in Hook, R. H. (ed.) *Fantasy and Symbol: Studies in Anthropological Interpretation*. New York: Academic Press, pp. 133–148.

Van Gennep, A. (1960) *The Rites of Passage*. London: Routledge.

Godelier, M. (2011) *The Metamorphoses of Kinship*. London: Verso.

Greer, J. (2020) "Prohibited Pigs and Prescribed Priestly Portions: Zooarchaeological Remains from Tel Dan and Questions Concerning Ethnicity and Priestly Traditions in the Hebrew Bible," in Altmann, P., Angelini, A., and Spiciarich, A. (eds) *Food Taboos and Biblical*

Prohibitions: Reassessing Archaeological and Literary Perspectives. Tübingen: Mohr Siebeck, pp. 73–85.

Harris, M. (1974) *Cows, Pigs, Wars, and Witches.* New York: Vintage Books.

Harris, M. (1985a) *Good to Eat: Riddles of Food and Culture.* Long Grove (IL): Waveland Press.

Harris, M. (1985b) *The Sacred Cow and the Abominable Pig: Riddles of Food and Culture.* New York: Simon and Schuster.

Hastorf, C. A. (2016) *The Social Archaeology of Food: Thinking about Eating from Prehistory to the Present.* Cambridge: Cambridge University Press.

Hawkes, C. (1954) "Wenner-Gren Foundation Supper Conference: Archeological Theory and Method: Some Suggestions from the Old World," *American Anthropologist, New Series,* 56(2), pp. 155–168.

Henrich, J. (2004) "Demography and Cultural Evolution: How Adaptive Cultural Processes Can Produce Maladaptive Losses: The Tasmanian Case," *American Antiquity,* 69, pp. 197–214.

Henrich, J. and Henrich, N. (2010) "The Evolution of Cultural Adaptations: Fijian Food Taboos Protect against Dangerous Marine Toxins," *Proceedings of the Royal Society B,* 277, pp. 3715–3724.

Héritier, F. (1979) "Symbolique de l'inceste et de sa prohibition," in Izard, M. and Smith, P. (eds) *La fonction symbolique.* Paris: Gallimard, pp. 209–243.

Hesse, B. and Wapnish, P. (1998) "Pig Use and Abuse in the Ancient Levant: Ethnoreligious Boundary-Building and Swine," in Nelson, S. (ed.) *Ancestors for the Pigs.* Philadelphia: University of Pennsylvania Museum of Archaeology and Anthropology, MASCA Research Papers in Science and Archaeology 15, pp. 123–135.

Hesse, B. and Wapnish, P. (2000) "Can Pig Remains Be Used for Ethnic Diagnosis in the Ancient Near East?" in Silberman, N. A. and Small, D. B. (eds) *The Archaeology of Israel: Constructing the Past, Interpreting the Present.* Sheffield: Sheffield Academic Press (Journal for the Study of the Old Testament Supplement Series 237), pp. 238–270.

Hodder, I. (1986) *Reading the Past.* Cambridge: Cambridge University Press.

Horton, D. R. (1979) "Tasmanian Adaptation," *Mankind.* Oxford: Blackwell, 12(1), pp. 28–34.

Horton, M. (1996) "Architecture: Materials, Functions and Evolution," in Horton, M. (ed.) *Shanga: The Archaeology of a Muslim Trading Community on the Coast of East Africa.* Nairobi: British Institute in Eastern Africa, pp. 224–242.

Horwitz, L. K., Gardeisen, A. M., Hitchcock, A. M., Louise A. (2017) "A Contribution to the Iron Age Philistine Pig Debate," in Lev-Tov, J., Hesse, P., and Gilbert, A. (eds) *The Wide Lens in Archaeology: Honoring*

Brian Hesse's Contributions to Anthropological Archaeology. Atlanta (GA): Lockwood Press, pp. 93–116.

Ijzereef, F. G. (1989) "Social Differentiation from Animal Bone Studies," in Serjeantson, D. and Waldron, T. (eds) *Diet and Crafts in Towns*. Oxford: BAR, pp. 41–53.

Jaffe, Y. (2023) *Food in Ancient China*. Cambridge University Press.

Jones, R. (1978) "Why Did the Tasmanians Stop Eating Fish," in Gould, R. (ed.) *Explorations in Ethnoarchaeology*. Santa Fe: University of New Mexico Press, Cambridge, pp. 11–47.

Jones, R. (1984) "Hunters and History: A Case Study from Western Tasmania," in Schrire, C., Eibl-Eibesfeldt, I., and Wiessner, P. W. (eds) *Past and Present in Hunter Gatherer Studies*. New York: Academic Press, pp. 27–65.

Jones, R. (1995) "Tasmanian archaeology: Establishing the Sequences," *Annual Review of Anthropology*. Annual Reviews 4139 El Camino Way, PO Box 10139, Palo Alto, CA 94303–0139, USA, 24(1), pp. 423–446.

Kahn, M. (1986) *Always Hungry, Never Greedy*. Cambridge: Cambridge University Press.

Khara, T., Riedy, C., and Ruby, M. B. (2020) "'We Have to Keep It a Secret' – The Dynamics of Front and Backstage Behaviours Surrounding Meat Consumption in India," *Appetite*, 149, p. 104615. https://doi.org/10.1016/j.appet.2020.104615.

King, J. (1785) *A Voyage to the Pacific Ocean, Vol. III*. London: H. Hughes. https://open.library.ubc.ca/collections/bcbooks/items/1.0342315.

Krämer, H. M. (2008) "'Not Befitting Our Divine Country': Eating Meat in Japanese Discourses of Self and Other from the Seventeenth Century to the Present," *Food and Foodways*. Taylor & Francis, 16(1), pp. 33–62.

Kusimba, C. M. (2023) *Swahili Worlds in Globalism*. Cambridge: Cambridge University Press.

Lawrence, F. (2013) "Horsemeat Scandal: The Essential Guide," *The Guardian*, 15 February 2013.

Lepowsky, M. A. (1985) "Food Taboos, Malaria and Dietary Change: Infant Feeding and Cultural Adaptation on a Papua New Guinea Island," *Ecology of Food and Nutrition*. Routledge, 16(2), pp. 105–126. https://doi.org/10.1080/03670244.1985.9990853.

Lev-Tov, J. (2012) "A Preliminary Report on the Late Bronze and Iron Age Faunal Assemblages from Tell es- Safi/Gath," in Maeir, A. (ed.) *Tell es-Safi /Gath I: Report on the 1996–2005 Seasons*. Harrassowitz. Ägypten und Altes Testament 69: Wiesbaden, pp. 589–612.

Lev-Tov, J. S. (2000) *Pigs, Philistines, and the Ancient Animal Economy of Ekron from the Late Bronze Age to the Iron Age II*. University of Tennessee, Knoxville.

Lev, M. and Barkai, R. (2016) "Elephants Are People, People Are Elephants: Human–Proboscideans Similarities as a Case for Cross Cultural Animal Humanization in Recent and Paleolithic Times," *Quaternary International*, 406, pp. 239–245. https://doi.org/10.1016/j.quaint.2015.07.005.

Lévi-Strauss, C. (1969) *The Elementary Structures of Kinship*. Boston, MA: Beacon Press.

Lisowski, M. (2019) *The Identification of Jewish Patterns of Food Preparation and Consumption: A Zooarchaeological Approach to the Medieval and Early Modern Evidence from Central Europe*. Unpublished PhD thesis, University of Sheffield.

Lyman, R. L. (1985) "Bone Frequencies: Differential Transport, in Situ Destruction, and the MGUI," *Journal of Archaeological Science*. Elsevier, 12(3), pp. 221–236.

Lyman, R. L. (2003) "The Influence of Time Averaging and Space Averaging on the Application of Foraging Theory in Zooarchaeology," *Journal of Archaeological Science*, 30, pp. 595–610.

Makarewicz, C. (2016) "Toward an Integrated Isotope Zooarchaeology," in Gruope, G. and McGlynn, G. C. (eds) *Isotopic Landscapes in Bioarchaeology*. Berlin: Springer, pp. 189–209.

Marett, R. R. (1909) *The Threshold of Religion*, 2nd Ed. London: Metheun.

Mead, M. (1937) *Tabu, Encyclopaedia of the Social Sciences, vol. 7*. London: The Macmillan.

Mead, M. (1978) "A Proposal: We Need Taboos on Sex at Work," *Redbook*, 150, pp. 31, 33, 38.

Meadow, R. H. (1980) "Animal Bones: Problems for the Archaeologist together with Some Possible Solutions," *Paléorient*, 6, pp. 65–77.

Mednick, S. (1962) "The Associative Basis of the Creative Process," *Psychological Review*. American Psychological Association, 69(3), p. 220–232.

Meigs, A. S. (1984) *Food, Sex, and Pollution*. New Brunswick: Rutgers University Press.

Melville, H. (1893) *Typee: A Narrative of a Four Months' Residence among the Native of a Valley of the Marqeusas Islands*. London: John Murray.

Meyer-Rochow, V. B. (2009) "Food Taboos: Their Origins and Purposes," *Journal of Ethnobiology and Ethnomedicine*, 5, p. 18.

Milgrom, J. (1998) *Leviticus 1–16*. New York: Anchor Bible.

Miller, M. J. et al. (2021) "Quinoa, Potatoes, and llamas Fueled Emergent Social Complexity in the Lake Titicaca Basin of the Andes," *Proceedings of the National Academy of Sciences*. National Academy of Sciences, 118(49), p. e2113395118.

Miller, S. (2004) *Disgust: The Gatekeeper Emotion*. New York: Routledge.

Milner, N., Craig, O. E., Bailey, G. N., Kristian, P., Søren H. (2004) "Something Fishy in the Neolithic? A Re-evaluation of Stable Isotope Analysis of Mesolithic and Neolithic Coastal Populations," *Antiquity*. Cambridge University Press, 78(299), pp. 9–22.

Milner, N., Craig, O. E., Bailey, G. N., Kristian, P., Søren H. (2006) "A Response to Richards and Schulting," *Antiquity*. Cambridge University Press, 80(308), pp. 456–458.

Morris, B. (1998) *The Power of Animals: An Ethnography*. Oxford: Berg.

Nemeroff, C. and Rozin, P. (1992) "Sympathetic Magical Beliefs and Kosher Dietary Practice: The Interaction of Rules and Feelings," *Ethos*. JSTOR, 20(1), pp. 96–115.

Papineau, D. and Heyes, C. (2006) "Rational or Associative? Imitation in Japanese quail," in *Rational Animals*. S. Hurley & M. Nudds (Eds.). Oxford: Oxford University Press, pp. 187–195.

Pavao-Zuckerman, B., Mayfield, Tracie Copperstone, Chance Foster, H. Thomas (2018) "'Horned Cattle and Pack Horses": Zooarchaeological Legacy Collections from the Unauthorized (and Unscreened) Spanish Fort," *Southeastern Archaeology*. Routledge, 37(3), pp. 190–203. https://doi.org/10.1080/0734578X.2018.1459133.

Peres, T. M. (2017) "Foodways Archaeology: A Decade of Research from the Southeastern United States," *Journal of Archaeological Research*. Springer, 25, pp. 421–460.

Perry-Gal, L., Ktalav, Inbar Nadav-Ziv, Liat, Haddad, Elie (2022) "Pigs in a Pit: An Unusual Find of Ritual Suid Exploitation in an Early Islamic Context at the Site of Tel Yavne, Israel," *Journal of Archaeological Science: Reports*, 43, p. 103462. https://doi.org/10.1016/j.jasrep.2022.103462.

Perry-Gal, L., Lieberman, T., and Uziel, J. (2024) "Ingestible Identity: Pigs in Pagan Ritual in Aelia Capitolina (Roman Jerusalem) between the Second Temple Period and Early Christianity," *Archaeological and Anthropological Sciences*, 16, p. 35.

Perry, R. B. (1926) *General Theory of Value*. New York: Longmans, Green.

Peters, J. and Schmidt, K. (2004) "Animals in the Symbolic World of PrePottery Neolithic Göbekli Tepe, Southeastern Turkey: A Preliminary Assessment," *Anthropozoologica*, 39, pp. 179–218.

Piaget, J. (1930) *The Child's Conception of Physical Reality*. London: Kegan Paul.

Politis, G. G. (2007) *Nukak: Ethnoarchaeology of an Amazonian People*. Walnut Creek: Left Coast Press.

Politis, G. G. (2016) "Bonescapes: Engaging People and Land with Animal Bones among South American Tropical Foragers," in Lovis, W. A. (ed.)

Marking the Land: Hunter-Gatherer Creation of Meaning in their Environment. London: Routledge, pp. 152–179.

Politis, G. G. and Saunders, N. J. (2002) "Archaeological Correlates of Ideological Activity: Food Taboos and Spirit-Animals in an Amazonian Hunter-Gatherer Society," in Miracle, C. P. T. and Milner, N. (eds) *Consuming Passions and Patterns of Consumption*. Cambridge: McDonald Institute for Archaeological Research, pp. 113–130.

Poole, K. (2013) "Horses for Courses? Religious Change and Dietary Shifts in Anglo-Saxon England," *Oxford Journal of Archaeology*. Wiley Online Library, 32(3), pp. 319–333.

Power, C. (2015) "Hadza Gender Rituals – Epeme and Maitoko – Considered as Counterparts," *Hunter Gatherer Research*, 1, pp. 333–358.

Price, M. D. (2021) *Evolution of a Taboo: Pigs and People in the Ancient Near East*. New York: Oxford University Press.

Price, M. D. (2022) "Food and Israelite Identity," in Fu, J., Shafer-Elliott, C., and Meyers, C. (eds) *T&T Clark Handbook of Food in the Hebrew Bible and Ancient Israel*. London: T&T Clark, pp. 423–463.

Price, M. D. and Hongo, H. (2020) "The Archaeology of Pig Domestication: Methods, Models, and Case Studies," *Journal of Archaeological Research*, 28, pp. 557–615.

Radcliffe-Brown, A. R. (1939) *Taboo*. Cambridge: Cambridge University Press.

Rautman, A. E. and Fenton, T. W. (2005) "A Case of Historic Cannibalism in the American West: Implications for Southwestern Archaeology," *American Antiquity*. Cambridge University Press, 70(2), pp. 321–341.

Reichel-Dolmatoff, G. (1978) "Desana Animal Categories, Food Restrictions, and the Concept of Color Energies," *Journal of Latin American Lore*, 4, pp. 243–291.

Rhodes, R. (1997) *Deadly Feasts: Tracking the Secrets of a Terrifying New Plague*. New York: Touchstone.

Rhyder, J. (2021) *Centralizing the Cult: The Holiness Legislation in Leviticus 17–26*. Tübingen: Mohr Siebeck.

Rhyder, J. (2023) "The Jewish Pig Prohibition from Leviticus to the Maccabees," *Journal of Biblical Literature*. Duke University Press, 142(2), pp. 221–241.

Richards, M. P. and Hedges, R. E. M. (1999) "A Neolithic Revolution? New Evidence of Diet in the British Neolithic," *Antiquity*. Cambridge University Press, 73(282), pp. 891–897.

Richards, M. P. and Schulting, R. J. (2006) "Touch Not the Fish: The Mesolithic-Neolithic Change of Diet and Its Significance," *Antiquity*. Cambridge University Press, 80(308), pp. 444–456.

Rosenblum, J.D. (2024). *Forbidden: A 3,000-Year History of Jews and the Pig*. New York: NYU Press.

Rosenblum, J. D. (2010) "'Why Do You Refuse to Eat Pork?': Jews, Food, and Identity in Roman Palestine," *The Jewish Quarterly Review*, 100, pp. 95–110.

Rosengren, K. S. and French, J. A. (2013) "Magical Thinking," in Taylor, M. (ed.) *The Oxford Handbook of the Development of Imagination*. New York: Oxford University Press, pp. 42–60.

Ross, E. (1978) "Food Taboos, Diet, and Hunting Strategy: The Adaptation to Animals in Amazon Cultural Ecology," *Current Anthropology*, 19, pp. 1–16.

Rozin, P., Haidt, Jonathan, McCauley, C., Imada, Sumio (1997) "Disgust: The Cultural Evolution of a Food-based Emotion," in Macbeth, H. (ed.) *Food Preference and Taste: Continuity and Change*. New York: Berghahn Books, pp. 65–82.

Rozin, P., Haidt, J., and McCauley, C. R. (2008) "Disgust," in Lewis, M., Haviland-Jones, J. M., and Barrett, L. F. (eds) *Handbook of Emotions*. New York: The Guilford Press, pp. 757–776.

Rozin, P., Markwith, M., and Nemeroff, C. (1992) "Magical Contagion Beliefs and Fear of AIDS," *Journal of Applied Social Psychology*. Wiley Online Library, 22(14), pp. 1081–1092.

Rozin, P., Markwith, M., and Ross, B. (1990) "The Sympathetic Magical Law of Similarity, Nominal Realism and Neglect of Negatives in Response to Negative Labels," *Psychological Science*. Los Angeles, CA: SAGE, 1(6), pp. 383–384.

Rozin, P., Markwith, M., and Stoess, C. (1997) "Moralization and Becoming a Vegetarian: The Transformation of Preferences into Values and the Recruitment of Disgust," *Psychological Science*, 8, pp. 67–73.

Russell, N. (2012) *Social Zooarchaeology: Humans and Animals in Prehistory*. Cambridge: Cambridge University Press.

Russell, N. (2018) "Neolithic Taboos in Anatolia and Southeast Europe," in Ivanova, M., Athanassov, Bogdan, Petrova, Vany, Takorova, Desislava, Stockhammer, Philipp W. (eds) *Social Dimensions of Food in the Prehistoric Balkans*. Oxford: Oxbow Books, pp. 14–30.

Sakurai, J. (2017) "Archaeology of Early-Modern Japan: Food, Rituals, and Taboos," in Habu, J., Lape, P. V., and Olsen, J. W. (eds) *Handbook of East and Southeast Asian Archaeology*. New York: Springer, pp. 677–694.

Saladié, P. and Rodríguez-Hidalgo, A. (2017) "Archaeological Evidence for Cannibalism in Prehistoric Western Europe: From Homo Antecessor to the Bronze Age," *Journal of Archaeological Method and Theory*, 24(4), pp. 1034–1071. https://doi.org/10.1007/s10816-016-9306-y.

Sanday, P. R. (1986) *Divine Hunger: Cannibalism as a Cultural System*. Cambridge: Cambridge University Press.

Sapir-Hen, L., Bar-Oz, Guy, Gadot, Yuval, Finkelstein, Israel (2013) "Pig Husbandry in Iron Age Israel and Judah," in Kamlah, J., Lichtenberger, A., and Witte, M. (eds) *Zeitschrift des Deutschen Palästine-Vereins*. Weisbaden: Harrassowitz Verlag, pp. 1–22.

Sapir-Hen, L. (2018) "Food, Pork Consumption, and Identity in Ancient Israel," *Near Eastern Archaeology*, 81, pp. 52–59.

Schoeninger, M. J. (2014) "Stable Isotope Analyses and the Evolution of Human Diets," *Annual Review of Anthropology*. Annual Reviews, 43(1), pp. 413–430.

Schwitzgebel, E. and Ellis, J. (2017) "Rationalization in Moral and Philosophical Thought," in Bonnefon, J.-F. and Trémolière, B. (eds) *Moral Inferences*. London: Routledge, pp. 170–190.

Scott, E. M. (1996) "Who Ate What? Archaeological Food Remains and Cultural Diversity," in Reitz, E. J., Newsom, L. A., and Scudder, S. J. (eds) *Case Studies in Environmental Archaeology: Interdisciplinary Contributions to Archaeology*. New York: Plenum Press, pp. 357–374.

Serjeantson, D. (2000) "Good to Eat and Good to Think with: Classifying Animals from Complex Sites," in Rowley-Conwy, P. A. (ed.) *Animal Bones, Human Societies*. Oxford: Oxbow Books, pp. 179–189.

Shimizu, A. (2010) "Meat-eating in the Kōjimachi District of Edo," in Rath, E. C. and Assmann, S. (eds) *Japanese Foodways, Past and Present*. Urbana: University of Illinois Press, pp. 92–107.

Simoons, F. J. (1961) *Eat Not This Flesh: Food Avoidances in the Old World*. Madison: University of Wisconsin Press.

Simoons, F. J. (1994) *Eat Not This Flesh: Food Avoidances in the Old World, 2nd Ed*. Madison University of Wisconsin Press.

Singh, M. and Henrich, J. (2020) "Why Do Religious Leaders Observe Costly Prohibitions? Examining Taboos on Mentawai Shamans," *Evolutionary Human Sciences*. Cambridge University Press, 2, p. e32.

Smith, C. (1999) "Dogs, Cats and Horses in the Scottish Medieval Town," in *Proceedings of the Society of Antiquaries of Scotland*, pp. 859–885.

Smith, W. R. (2017) *The Religion of the Semites*. London: Routledge.

Sperber, D. (1997) "Intuitive and Reflective Beliefs," *Mind & Language*, 12, pp. 67–83.

Speth, J. D. (2009) *The Paleoanthropology and Archaeology of Big-Game Hunting: Protein, Fat, or Politics?* New York: Springer.

Steiner, F. (1956) *Taboo*. London: Cohen and West.

Testart, A. (1991) *Des Mythes et des Croyances: Esquisse d/une Théorie Générale*. Paris: Maison des Sciences de l'Homme.

Thomas, J. (2003) "Thoughts on the 'Repacked' Neolithic Revolution," *Antiquity*, 77, pp. 67–74.

Turner, V. (1964) "Betwixt and between: The Liminal Period in Rites de Passage," *The Proceedings of the American Ethnological Society*, 1964, pp. 4–20.

Turner, V. (1967) *The Forest of Symbols: Aspects of Ndembu Ritual*. Ithaca (NY): Cornell University Press.

Twiss, K. C. (2006) "A Modified Boar Skull from Çatalhöyük," *Bulletin of the American Schools of Oriental Research*, 342, pp. 1–12.

Twiss, K. C. (2008) "Transformations in an Early Agricultural Society: Feasting in the Southern Levantine Pre-Pottery Neolithic," *Journal of Anthropological Archaeology*, 27, pp. 418–442.

Twiss, K. C. (2019) *The Archaeology of Food: Identity, Politics, and Ideology in the Prehistoric and Historic Past*. Cambridge University Press.

Valenzuela-Lamas, S., Valenzuela-Suau, L., Saula, O., Colet, A., Mercadal, O., Subiranas, C. and Nadal, J. (2014) "Shechita and Kashrut: Identifying Jewish Populations through Zooarchaeology and Taphonomy: Two Examples from Medieval Catalonia (North-Eastern Spain)," *Quaternary International*. Elsevier, 330, pp. 109–117.

Valeri, V. (2000) *The Forest of Taboos: Morality, Hunting, and Identity among the Huaulu of the Moluccas*. Madison: University of Wisconsin Press.

Vermeersch, S. *et al.* (2021) "Animal Husbandry from the Middle Bronze Age through the Iron Age in the Shephelah – Faunal Remains from the New Excavations at Lachish," *Archaeological and Anthropological Sciences*, 13(3), p. 38. https://doi.org/10.1007/s12520-021-01289-1.

Villa, P. (1992) "Cannibalism in Prehistoric Europe," *Evolutionary Anthropology: Issues, News, and Reviews*. Wiley Online Library, 1(3), pp. 93–104.

Walker, B. L. (2001) "Commercial Growth and Environmental Change in Early Modern Japan: Hachinohe's Wild Boar Famine of 1749," *Journal of Asian Studies*, 60(2), pp. 329–351.

Warter, J. W. (ed.) (1856) *Selections from the Letter of Robert Southey, Vol. III*. London: Longman, Brown, Green, Longmans, and Roberts.

Webb, M. C. (1965) "The Abolition of the Taboo System in Hawaii," *The Journal of the Polynesian Society*. JSTOR, 74(1), pp. 21–39.

Weber, M. (2019) *Economy and Society: A New Translation*. Cambridge, MA: Harvard University Press.

Weil, K. (2007) "They Eat Horses, Don't They? Hippophagy and Frenchness," *Gastronomica*. University of California Press, 7(2), pp. 44–51.

White, T. E. (1952) 'Observations on the Butchering Technique of Some Aboriginal Peoples: I," *American Antiquity*. Cambridge University Press, 17(4), pp. 337–338.

Whitfield, J. T., Pako, W. H., Collinge, J., Alpers, M.P. (2008) "Mortuary Rites of the South Fore and Kuru," *Philosophical Transactions of the Royal Society B: Biological Sciences*, 363, pp. 3721–3724.

Willey, G. R. and Phillips, P. (1958) *Method and Theory in Archaeology*. Chicago: University of Chicago Press.

Wilson, B. and Edwards, P. (1993) "Butchery of Horse and Dog at Witney Palace, Oxfordshire, and the knackering and Feeding of Meat to Hounds during the Post-medieval Period," *Post-Medieval Archaeology*. Taylor & Francis, 27(1), pp. 43–56.

Winchcombe, R. (2023) "The Limits of Disgust: Eating the Inedible during Jamestown's Starving Time," *Global Food History*. Taylor & Francis, pp. 1–23.

Woodburn, J. (1964) 'The Social Organization of the Hadza of North Tanganyika. Unpublished PhD thesis, Cambridge University. Unpublished PhD thesis, Cambridge University.

Wundt, W. (1921) *The Elements of Folk Psychology*. London: Allen and Unwin.

Zvelebil, M. (2000) "Fat Is a Feminist Issue: On Ideology, Diet and Health in Hunter-Gatherer Societies," in Donald, M. and Hurcombe, L. (eds) *Gender and Material Culture in Archaeological Perspective*. New York: Palgrave Macmillan, pp. 209–221.

Cambridge Elements

Archaeology of Food

Katheryn C. Twiss
Stony Brook University, New York

Katheryn C. Twiss is an archaeologist who studies ancient foodways in order to learn about social structures in the prehistoric and early historic past. Her primary areas of expertise are southwest Asian prehistory, zooarchaeology, animal management and symbolism, and life in early farming communities. Dr. Twiss wrote *The Archaeology of Food: Identity, Politics, and Ideology in the Prehistoric and Historic Past* (Cambridge University Press, 2019) and edited *The Archaeology of Food And Identity* (Southern Illinois University, 2007). She has published on topics ranging from feasting in early farming villages to Mesopotamian ceremonialism.

Alexandra Livarda
Catalan Institute of Classical Archaeology

Alexandra Livarda studies human-plant interactions through time and what they reveal about agronomy, commerce, social structures, perceptions, and identities in the past, but also how these may impact the present. She specialises in archaeobotany, Aegean archaeology, Roman commerce and is developing new methodological tools for the identification of past agricultural practices. Dr. Livarda has directed or (co)/directed archaeobotanical research in several projects, including some of the most emblematic sites in the Aegean, such as the Little Palace at Knossos and Lefkandi. She has published on a range of topics from the emergence of agriculture to the development of tastes and food commerce in the historic past.

About the Series

Elements in the Archaeology of Food showcase the vibrancy and intellectual diversity of twenty-first century archaeological research into food. Volumes reveal how food archaeology not only illuminates ancient political manoeuvres, social networks, risk management strategies, and luxurious pleasures, but also engages with modern heritage management, health, and environmental conservation strategies.

Cambridge Elements ≡

Archaeology of Food

Elements in the Series

Food in Ancient China
Yitzchak Jaffe

How Urbanism Changes Foodways
Monica L. Smith

The Behavioral Ecology of Food: Bridging the Archaeological and the Contemporary
Elic M. Weitzel and Natalie D. Munro

Food Taboos in Archaeology
Max Price

A full series listing is available at: www.cambridge.org/EIAF

For EU product safety concerns, contact us at Calle de José Abascal, 56–1°,
28003 Madrid, Spain or eugpsr@cambridge.org.

www.ingramcontent.com/pod-product-compliance
Lightning Source LLC
LaVergne TN
LVHW011855060526
838200LV00054B/4346